Vertical World

Conversations with Today's Masters of Rock

Katie Brown

FALCON GUIDE®

GUILFORD, CONNECTICUT
HELENA, MONTANA
AN IMPRINT OF THE GLOBE PEQUOT PRESS

Falcon, FalconGuide, and Chockstone are registered trademarks of Morris Book Publishing, LLC.

Text design: Casey Shain
Interior photo credits appear on page ix.

Library of Congress Cataloging-in-Publication Data
Brown, Katie.
  Vertical world : conversations with today's masters of rock / Katie Brown.
— 1st ed.
     p. cm.
   ISBN-13: 978-0-7627-4008-6
   ISBN-10: 0-7627-4008-6
   1. Mountaineers—Biography. 2. Mountaineering. I. Title.
GV199.9.B755 2006
796.5220922—dc22
  [B]
                                                                        2006016637

Manufactured in China
First Edition/First Printing

To buy books in quantity for corporate use
or incentives, call **(800) 962–0973, ext. 4551,**
or e-mail **premiums@GlobePequot.com.**

Contents

Tommy Caldwell cruxing
on *Grand Ol' Opry* (5.14a),
The Monastery, Colorado

"Sport climbing saved climbing." I heard that said one time while cragging at a newly bolted cliff in 1989. The speaker sat in the dirt while holding a rope for another climber working the moves on an overhanging route. He had noted that mainstream climbing of the mid-1980s had reached—with a few notable exceptions—a hiatus. Nothing it seemed, except the sport phenomenon, had rocked American climbing quite like the earlier breakthroughs of the 1960s "Golden Age" of Yosemite, or free-climbing revolution of the 1970s. The late 1970s through the early 1980s had seen America's climbing standards pushed—from the world's first 5.13 by Tony Yaniro, to the ascent of *Midnight Lightning*, and outrageous feats like Bachar's free solo of the Nabisco Wall in Yosemite—but the real transformation came from Europe and places like Smith Rock. In those areas the whole-sale application of rappel-placed fixed gear would ultimately change the way *everybody* climbed.

Only five years earlier such a claim as my friend's would have been akin to sacrilege and might warrant, at the very minimum, a verbal rebuke. In some circles the acrimony surrounding what was then an "ethical" issue might have even led to blows. Such was the controversy generated by and the frightening acceleration of that genre's popularity.

Truth be told, were my friend to gaze into a crystal ball back in 1989, he might have stated, "sport climbing *and bouldering* saved climbing." Indeed the former so fed the popularity of the latter that, by the mid-1990s, boulder-ing was the most popular pursuit within the climbing game. Today bouldering has energized all facets of the sport in no small part due to its explosion of extreme difficulty, athleticism, and engaging social dynamic. For a parallel we can look at the skateboarding surge of the 1970s when groups of kids threw off uptight strictures and started doing tricks for the sake of doing tricks. Like the boulderers of today, those kids were the unwitting torchbearers of new-school difficulty. It was their efforts, attitudes, and originality that took a ridiculous pastime and transformed it into a focal point of youth culture. Sitting in the dirt in 1989, we knew little of how deep and pervasive this revolution would become. Only now, almost twenty years later, can we gauge the impact with a historical yardstick.

Nick O'Connell's *Beyond Risk: Conversations with Climbers* was written in 1993. O'Connell's book, a compendium of climber interviews, is in some ways the forerunner to *Vertical World*. Greg Child, noting the changes in equipment, technique, and attitude of the preceding six decades, wrote in *Beyond Risk*'s foreword, "Climbing has evolved rapidly over the last hundred years. A climber of the 1930s, or earlier, would be startled to see the shape of climbing in the 1990s."

From my experiences I can say that I am startled to see how the shape of climbing has changed in the last *fifteen* years. The differences are subtle yet potent. In that decade and a half, no one invented truly revolutionary tools or techniques. However, over that same period, the attitudes, standards, and, most significantly, sociological shifts forever altered the map of our sport. So profound are these changes that it is not uncommon for a child only a year into his or her climbing career to surpass the achievements that formerly required a decade of blood, sweat, and tears.

The rock gym is the crucible for these tremendous changes. Though the first gyms were born smack dab amidst the Reagan era, it was the proliferation of these indoor climbing facilities by the mid-1990s that so affected our sport. These indoor facilities created year-round training zones—no longer did one have to quit his or her job or school to climb. They also tapped into a wider genetic pool of talent and cast a wide net throughout middle-class suburbia. No longer was climbing the fringe lifestyle as in my era; it became something that children and teenagers could easily share with friends and family. The gyms brought the mountains to suburbia. They have grown so popular that today you'll find plastic mountains in every major urban area of the United States.

The seeds of this revolution are bearing fruit not just in the specialized niches of plastic, sport climbing, or bouldering. The effects are being seen with impressive clarity in the traditional bastions of trad, big wall (free and aid), ice/mixed, and alpine rock climbing.

In the following chapters Katie Brown interviews nine climbers who have made significant contributions to the sport. "These contributions will stand the test of time," she says. Her intent—besides inaugurating a career as an author—is to portray the leading activists of the new generation. She's chosen three women and six men representing America's current cutting edge of bouldering, sport, trad, big wall free, and alpine rock climbing.

It's worth noting that almost half the climbers profiled here began their careers on plastic. Every one of these outstanding climbers, whether they choose to emphasize or downplay bolt clipping, have embraced sport climbing at some point either as an end in itself or as a significant part of their training. Lucky for us readers, Katie rubbed shoulders and/or competed with most of the climbers profiled herein. We benefit from the fact that, as Katie says, "I was there. I climbed with them for over a decade and grew up with them."

What else makes Katie qualified to write this book? First off, she's no lightweight. In fact I recall that in 1999, when tasked with painstakingly sorting through candidates for *Climbing*'s millennium issue, I chose Katie Brown as "Best Female Climber of the Millennium." The teenager emerged from a field including fly-by-night rising stars and living legends. I did so because not only was Katie the most successful competitor on the female World Cup circuit, but she pulled off several coups by *onsighting* not one but two routes that, at the time, represented the *limits* of female *redpointing*.

Katie's incendiary climbing career first gained public attention when she won the Junior World Championships in 1995. She went on to win the coveted Arco Rockmaster twice. She also placed second at the prominent Serre Chevalier and won a World Cup event in Besancon in 1999. She also won the much-hyped X Games, not once but three times.

On rock, Katie made headlines in 1996 when she onsighted *Convicted* (5.13a) in the cavernous, arm-blasting Mother Lode of the Red River Gorge. She was then fourteen. Preferring onsights to projecting, Katie's top redpoints shadowed her maximum flash abilities.

In October 1999 she flashed a route on the immaculate limestone of Siurana, Spain, called *Hydrophobia*. The route, completed with draws in place and a scrap of beta, was rated 5.14a. That feat placed Katie among four others—all men, who, at the time, had flashed a similar grade. Though *Hydrophobia* was later downgraded to 5.13d, one has to question the objectivity of the grade, especially given Katie's slight stature and limited reach. What's unarguable is that her onsight was no fluke, for *Hydrophobia* came on the heels of another groundbreaking effort—an onsight of *Omaha Beach* (5.13d) in the Red River Gorge.

But that being said, it took quitting climbing to develop the other component that makes Katie so eminently qualified to write this book. In 1999 Katie escaped the gravitas of child climbing star to attend school. There, far from the expectations heaped on a climbing prodigy, she discovered a penchant for literature—and writing. Her first published pieces have been met with acclaim and controversy.

Two years after dropping out, Katie reemerged, this time as a force in trad climbing. In 2005 she freed the West Face of the Leaning Tower, a Grade V, big wall rated 5.13b, A0, in Yosemite. Her partner was no less than climbing legend Lynn Hill. Hill says, "Katie is a woman now, not the girl I remember. And she's chosen to learn the trad stuff."

Whatever her future goals may be in climbing, Katie will continue to inspire on and off the rock. She hopes that *Vertical World* will provide young climbers a true picture of the legacy they inherit. She also hopes to inspire a new generation to reach further than, "the purple taped route at the local gym."

—Pete Takeda
Boulder, Colorado

Acknowledgments

I would like to say thank you to all the climbers. Thank you for sharing your time with me, and for sharing yourself with a whole generation of young climbers who look up to you. By doing so I think you will help climbers everywhere understand what it is all about, why we climb, and why we love it. An immense thank you also to the photographers who generously contributed to the making of this book. It would not be what it is without your photos. And lastly, thanks to Sonnie Trotter, my idea man.

Photo Credits

p. i, 63, 64, 123, 128 © Jimmy Chin; p. iii, xiv, 5, 9, 11, 12, 15, 16, 78, 80, 83, 84, 87, 89, © Tim Kemple; p. iv, xii–xiii, 20, 23, 24, 25, 26, 28–29, 33, 35, 40, 43, 45, 46, 49, 53, 133, 146, 149, 151, 152, 155, 157, 159, 162 © Corey Rich/Aurora Photos; p. x, 94, 103 © Chris Goplerud; p. 2, 6–7 © Boone Speed; p. 36, 60, 137, 141 © Dean Fidelman; p. 39 © Sonnie Trotter; p. 51, 55, 148 © Topher Donahue/Alpinecreative; p. 58, 61, 67, 71, 72, 75, 112, 114, 117, 121, 124–25, 126 © Eric Perlman; p. 68–69, 118 © Whit Richardson; p. 81 © Alyrene Dorey; p. 97, 99, 100–101, 104 © Kelly Cordes; p. 107, 108, 110–11 © Jonathan Copp; p. 130, 135, 138 © PatitucciPhoto/Aurora Photos.

Josh Wharton getting bold in the Black Canyon of the Gunnison, Colorado

Inspiration is that which stimulates

us. When we are inspired we are motivated to "make" or create something. From the first day that I climbed, I was inspired. For the first couple of years, I mostly sat on the sidelines, watching others more skilled than I. I watched them and in turn was inspired to learn how to move on the rock with the ease that these people did. I was lucky, though. I had the opportunity from an early age to climb in the presence of some of the world's best. I sat in a dusty climbing gym at the age of fourteen, watching Francois Legrand, Robyn Erbesfield, Christian Griffith, Lynn Hill, and others as they practiced their craft. In addition to watching, I listened—too shy to say anything. My shyness, however, gave me the opportunity to see and hear them, not as figures in a magazine but as real people with tangible and valuable lessons to teach.

Several years later I realized that some of the people I had grown up with had become the climbers who were inspiring a whole new generation. The climbers in this book are my peers, but they are also incredibly talented athletes, role models, and amazing people. I knew that if given the opportunity, they would also have amazing advice and inspiration to offer. Not every fourteen-year-old, however, has the option of watching and listening to them in person. They are left with a magazine, a glossy photo, and someone else's perception of these people to read about.

What I envisioned for this book, then, was for some of the world's best to have the opportunity to inspire other climbers—young and old—with their own words, their own personality, their own advice. The words in this book are the climbers' own.

In addition, these climbers have all accomplished significant "firsts." They have advanced the sport and set new standards. Fifteen years ago many of the feats performed by these nine athletes were thought to be virtually impossible, unthinkable. Today, however, a whole new realm is opening up, making us wonder what will be possible in another fifteen years. These accomplishments are all things that can never be taken away. They will stand the test of time and deserve to be documented. Years down the road this book might be pulled off a parent's dusty shelf, and another young person will be held in awe by what these climbers did.

So if while reading this, you were inspired by all the climbers, or just one in particular, then I have done my job.

Tommy Caldwell enjoying a day of cragging at The Cookie Cliff, Yosemite National Park, California

Since his start in climbing, Dave has climbed **more** 5.14s than anyone else in the world.

Dave Graham has more energy than anyone I have ever met. He has not only a voracious appetite for climbing, but one for conversation as well. Dave is of medium height with an unbelievably wiry build and looks built more for marathon running than for climbing. He has dark hair and dark eyes that seem to continually dance in excitement.

Dave speaks in short, rapid-fire, stream-of-consciousness sentences, and when listening, one can actually hear, tangibly, how one thought leads to the next, to the next, to the next. . . .

Dave started climbing at fourteen with friend and also well-known climber Luke Parady. Dave and Luke were in a middle school band together, and he relates how Luke continually missed practice to go climbing. Eventually Dave became interested, and after trying it once, was instantly hooked. Before climbing, Dave had been involved in other sports, like hockey and skiing, but his thin stature always inhibited him from excelling. Climbing, however, didn't necessarily require size and brute strength, and he quickly learned that what other climbers could muscle through, he often could finesse through with technique and balance.

Since his start in climbing, Dave has climbed more 5.14s than anyone else in the world. He has both repeated and established routes around the world. The number exceeds one hundred, and Dave doesn't appear to be anywhere near stopping. In addition, he has established and/or repeated some of the world's hardest boulder problems. Some of his most noteworthy ascents include *Action Directe* (5.14d), *The Fly* (14d), *Bain de Sang* (14d), *Dreamtime* (V15), and *New Base Line* (V15). So what lies behind Dave's motivation? Well, it just seems to be who he is.

The Interview . . .

What did you play in your band?

Guitar. We played at school dances and stuff. We were totally ostracized. People thought we were weird. We weren't psyched on the system, and we expressed that in our music, so we got really dirty looks from teachers. But it was really fun, because at fourteen we played at the older kids' prom. We got to spread our propaganda and show a different perspective.

What did you like about climbing?

I liked figuring things out, and that I could never do it the same way as anyone else. Other people could just pull themselves around, but I was never strong like that, so I had to figure out other ways. And I always wanted to try and do everything possible, even from the beginning. In the gym I'd do the yellow route, so then I'd want to do the black route, then the blue route. Pretty quickly, though, Luke and I got bored of the gym and started climbing outside, in a quarry, and then we got superpsyched—climbing outside, having epics. That first year was a really funny year. We'd go to these really random spots and find ourselves trying to climb thirty-year-old routes. There wasn't much development in the Maine climbing scene at the time, so pretty soon we had done everything there was to do, and we had to start putting up our own stuff.

So how did you and Luke meet Joe? In the magazines you were always portrayed as an inseparable trio.

Well, Joe was one of the only other psyched people in that region. He was from New Hampshire, but I actually met Joe out West, and we started hanging out and just doing crazy shit. Joe was a little bit older than us, so he had a car, and we basically leeched onto him. Then Joe leeched onto us on that level—he moved to Portland while we were still in high school to go to art school, so we just hung out with him because, hell, we hated all the high school shit and we were very aware of the fact that we had someone else to hang out with. That definitely encouraged the whole process of doing things together.

You said the first time you went climbing outside was at a quarry in Portland. How'd you hear about that?

It's pretty much the only climbing area in Portland. There's a 12a, some 5.10s, and a 5.9 slab. At the time we were really into it, but it was really scary and horribly protected, so it got old pretty fast. We started going to a place called Shag Crag after that, and it had really cool 5.11s, 5.12s, and a couple of 5.13s. Shag Crag had really crazy granite routes and is still one of my favorite places to climb. It's beautiful.

Did you put up any routes there?

Yeah. It's funny because we graded them all 13b, and now they're all 13d or 14a.

What do you think you got out of climbing so much with the same partners?

It was really me and Luke back then. We climbed together all the time, and then eventually, around sixteen or seventeen, I took a trip without Luke. That's when our lives started going in different directions. He started to be more focused on school, and I decided that I just wanted to rock climb as much as I could. Up until that point, though, we climbed a lot together and influenced each other's climbing. Luke would do something, so I'd want to try it. And I'd eventually do it. And vice versa. Luke would be like, "Fuck. Dave did it. He's skinny. How'd that happen? I'm gonna do it." And he'd do it. So it was always us competing like that. But Luke was always the stronger one, so I'd have to find an entirely different way of doing everything. It was fun climbing with Luke, because he's a really different climber than me. He's a big, burly kid, and I can't do that ever. I still can't do that, unfortunately.

DAVE GRAHAM

Did you guys find Rumney, or was it already developed?

Rumney was developed by a group called Team Tough. They were this superfunny group of Massachusetts locals and New Hampshire people who had been climbing there forever. We were inspired by them, and they'd always turn us on to projects. They had bolted so many things that hadn't been done, so they'd tell us to try them and we'd slowly tick them off. After we discovered Rumney, that was pretty much the only place we'd go. We could really motivate each other. We had cars, we didn't have parents around, and we just climbed, all the time.

Dave Graham

Height: 5 feet, 10 inches

Weight: 132 pounds

Date of Birth: 11/10/81

Current Hometown: Nomad

Age of First Climb: 14

Approximate Number of Days Per Year Spent Climbing: 300

Hardest Climb: Coupe de Grace (15a??)

Favorite Climbing Area: Planet Earth

When did you do your first 5.14?

When I was fifteen, I think. Sixteen? It had been a year and a half after I started climbing, so . . . it was a route called *The Present*, in St. George, Utah. I did it in two tries. It was really funny, because I couldn't climb 13b if it was steep, and I did that one in two tries.

Why? Because it was lower angle or something?

Crimpy face climbing and technical. It took Luke ten tries, and it was a riot. It was the most random shit ever. Everybody thought it was fucked. It was weird, truly. I couldn't climb very hard back then. I had been to Rifle, and I think the hardest thing I did was 13a or something. We were on our second road trip ever, and I had a wild idea to drive up to St. George. I had heard it was cool and had seen a photo of Boone Speed on a 5.14 that I wanted to try. Everyone was telling me that I should try the 13bs first and do something productive before going and trying a 14a. But then I did it. And that was the beginning of climbing lots of hard routes.

And how many 5.14s have you done since then?

I don't know. I don't know that number, but it would have to be over seventy-five.

Have you ever counted them?

I count, but it's hard. I'm always downgrading them. It could be over a hundred I suppose, because I don't count 14as as much. The quantity, though, is not

Dave looking to add to his list of
5.14s, Black and Tan Wall, Utah

Everyone was telling me that I should **try the** 13bs **first and do** something **productive before going and trying a** 14a. **But then** I did it.

important. I'm into finding really mythical routes, and that's why I've stayed in Europe most of the time—there are a lot there. Some routes just have a certain aura, and I've never been into just doing stuff for the sake of doing it. I mean, I could climb a hell of a lot more 5.14s, but I've always been into picking specific routes.

What kind of routes inspire you or draw your attention?

That's a hard question. It's very personal, you know? It's very much about what I personally am intrigued by. If it's beautiful, if the line is interesting, if it's a crazy piece of rock, if it just looks fun. I don't like chipped routes, for instance. They don't look fun.

Do you think you tend to pick routes that suit your style?

No, I actually pick routes that aren't my style. Because that's my whole deal—trying to do things that I can't do.

Are you ever scared?

I'm horrified of rock climbing. All the time. I bolt routes but hate hanging on the rope. I'm always looking up thinking, "Gawd, I hate this. I want to be on the ground." I've been bolting a lot of routes these days, and I scare the shit out of myself. I have to organize everything, and if I'm supposed to do one of something I'll do two. When it comes to doing things like rappelling and climbing, I'm always scared.

How long do you think you can continue at the level that you're at?

Oh forever I hope, in terms of discovery. I never train or anything, and I feel like I'm still improving. It's all about motivation for me. If I'm really psyched about something and really want to do it, then I'll climb really well. I'll do something that I always thought would be really hard, and it'll surprise me because I won't have done anything different trainingwise. For example, the last couple of years I haven't been as psyched on climbing, and I haven't been doing anything, but recently I've gotten psyched again, and I'm climbing way better all of a sudden.

And what do you think has changed your motivation recently?

Not being solo, not being nomadic. For a long time I felt very castaway and ostracized from the whole world and the United States.

So you're more psyched living in one place?

I used to not know what I was doing, what I was going to do, or how it was going to work. But now I envision a future. It's had a lot to do with having a relationship, I think. That had a big effect on me, because I finally have something that matters to me other than climbing. I really hated being alone, but I traveled alone for years in Europe—I mean, at least I learned the

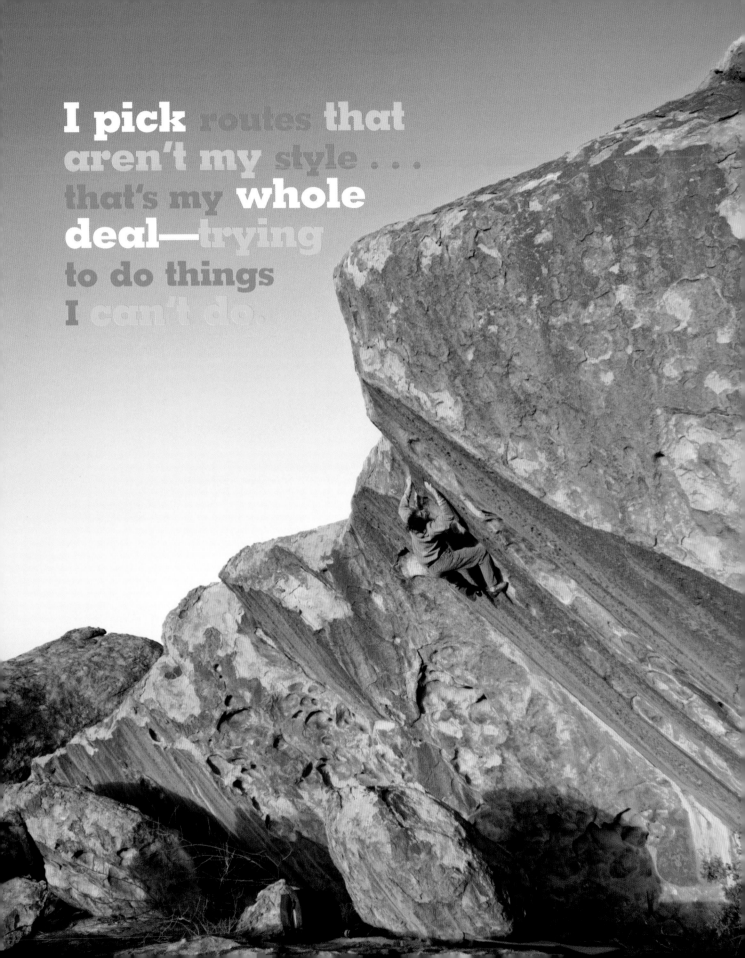

I pick routes that aren't my style . . . that's my whole deal—trying to do things I can't do.

language and how to deal with things on my own. But it got really tiring.

This year, though, I've been able to do some really hard boulders. Things I used to not have the attention span for—because I was always so frustrated with what was going on, who to go climbing with, where to go climbing, where to sleep that night, etcetera. And also I had a hard time coming to terms with being a "professional climber," whatever that means. It was hard for me to be in that world and figure out how to deal with it. I was always more of a "fuck-you" type and didn't want to perform, but I still had that inside of me—feeling like performing was necessary to survive. It was always this horrible paradox of not wanting to perform, yet thinking it was necessary. For example, when I was seventeen I went to Mount Charleston and climbed a lot of routes, and people were impressed, which I thought was ironic. People never took me seriously before I went to Mount Charleston, and I thought

that was so dumb. I had put up a lot of cool, natural routes in Rumney, but people were always skeptical about them. Then I go do a few horrible, chipped routes in Charleston, and everyone suddenly thinks I'm so strong. I hated that, because it wasn't true. I wasn't really strong. I'm still not. I figure things out and do them, but I'm not—I mean I've climbed a lot with Chris, and he does some crazy shit. Like fucking up a V6 and doing it the V14 way. People don't stare at me like that. I might look really weak on the V6, but I do it. That's the deal. I've never fit into the professional climber mold—especially since I didn't like comps either.

What was it about comps that you didn't like?

I thought it was dumb. It doesn't mean anything, because if the route setters throw a bunch of crimps up on the wall, I'll win. And if they put up a bunch of slopers, I'll

More Climbers to Watch

Emily Harrington

Date of Birth: 8/17/86

Years Climbing: 10

Hometown: Boulder, Colorado

Known For: First woman to climb 5.14 at Rifle Mountain Park

Shaking out on *Psychadelic*
(5.14d), Gorilla Cliffs, Utah

Dave sending pitch two of *Jumbo Pumping Hate* (5.14a), Mount Clark, California

lose. And that's dumb to me. That's not rock climbing, that's not a test of skill, that's a test to see how specialized everyone is.

Why did you end up moving to Europe?

I felt very out of joint with the United States. Leaving the U.S. was essential for me to figure out who I was. I didn't feel like I could be myself here. I felt like there was too much pressure to conform to a certain personality type and what society says you should be like. I felt like people weren't themselves in the United States. Everybody was really blinded by society and culture, and they couldn't really discover themselves. I didn't like seeing everybody trying so hard to "make it."

I'm interested in talking about things and ideas, but people just think I talk too much. My whole generation in general is not interested in what I have to say. Even now I can't talk to Joe. I bore the shit out of him. Nobody has the energy to talk or listen, and I just thought that if I traveled, maybe there were other people like me out there. So I went to France and really enjoyed it. I met a couple of people who were really into talking about things, and at the same time I started getting into exploration. It was great, because it was hard being a climber in the States. I was always the weird climber. Everybody made fun of me a lot, and I was sick of it.

What did they make fun of you about?

Just the way I climb. I mean you go to Rifle, get that kind of shit, and get really sick of it. "Dude, you ever eat?" Or "Why are you so skinny?" "Why do you talk so much?" I just felt completely misunderstood and thought, "I'll be damned. That's not necessary to put myself through that." So initially I started developing my own stuff in the States, like going to Chaos Canyon—nobody there except a few really cool friends to climb with.

I really started getting into traveling even while I was still in the States, and doing things that were less "in." I was always disgusted by how things were so "cool." Everybody was supercool, and I never got it. People are all trying to fit into the world that they live in. They're trying to be accepted. And I was always so baffled at how they couldn't just be happy with the way they were. Nobody says, "That's a *sick* boulder." Everybody's like, "Huh. That's cool I guess." It's not cool to be excited; it's not cool to talk, to ramble. It's not cool to be happy. And that's boring. I want to be excited, amazed by boulders, their shapes, their lines, the scenery. I'd rather be climbing alone than with people who are cool. It's a true excitement that I think is lost in our whole culture.

Do you think you'll ever move back to the States?

Yeah. I'm going to travel for the next year with my girlfriend, Lila. I hope it works, to be honest, because we're both very independent people, and I would find it really bad if something like the world could take all our attention away from each other. But we're planning on taking a yearlong travel through the States.

DAVE GRAHAM

What do you think is one of the fundamental differences between American climbers and European climbers?

One of the main differences is that their parents climbed. They're a generation ahead of us. Rock climbing is a very powerful thing. It can be negative, or quite positive. It's amazing how much climbing influences people's lives, and in Europe it's been demonstrated. Climbing is a very cultivated, rich part of their culture. There are sixty-year-old couples rappelling next to you, and they've been climbing their whole life. Also, young people are introduced to it in a completely different fashion than we are. Rather than being taken to the rock gym after school, kids learn to climb outdoors with their family. Certain people in America have that experience, but it's a tiny, tiny culture. Tommy had it, for instance. In Europe so many people have climbing integrated into their lives. I think it's much further along in terms of really experiencing the richness of climbing.

When you were younger, who did you look up to or draw inspiration from?

Well first it was Chris Sharma. Still is, really. He's the one doing things that I didn't think were possible. I learn so much from watching him. What's happening, physically, that's making it possible for him to do that move? I think you, even, were an inspiration, to be honest. My first experiences rock climbing were of Chris Sharma on the cover and you all over the inside. I got to look at people my age rock climbing, and I thought that was crazy.

On another level, Luke inspired me. He always did really cool things, right next to me. My best friend climbed really hard. And I climbed really hard because we climbed together. I don't think I would have been able to do that alone. Luke was probably the most inspiring person to me. I learned a lot from climbing with him.

Was it a goal when you first started climbing to do 5.14?

No. I wanted to climb everything. Anything that looked cool I was fascinated by. People would tell me that it was really hard, but I didn't care and I'd try anyway. It came down to a never ending curiosity for me. And also I was psyched to challenge myself. I just wanted to see if I could do things. It's never about climbing a certain number. I was always fascinated by the figuring out, not the doing.

What really screwed me all up, though, was feeling like I had to do things. As soon as I started doing things, I got all this respect that I never had. *Action Directe,* for example. I climbed that just for me. It was something that I wanted to do because it was *the* legendary route of the world. But then all of a sudden people treated me differently, like I had proved myself to them or something. It didn't take much longer to do than some projects I had done, but people thought the projects were nothing. *Action Directe* was everything, and I thought people must be so short-sighted to think that.

Dave on the first ascent of *Over the Rainbow* (V9), Zion National Park, Utah

Was there any route that was your favorite or the most challenging for you?

Oh wow. I love so many routes, but then there's some that I *really* love. Particularly this one in Switzerland. It's on a beautiful wall above an alpine lake. It was a Beat Kammerlander route, and I think I love that route because of the time and place that I climbed it. I had just made this horrible video, *Autoroute,* and I was not psyched. There was a lot of pressure, and I remember being superpsyched on having something that felt like it was just mine. It was my style, almost as if it was made exactly for me. I climbed it over the course of three rainy days, so by the time I did it, the route was a swath of dryness, the only thing on the wall that wasn't soaking wet. For me it was a very pull-your-shit-together experience, and I found in myself that I really could. It was one of the few times that rock climbing has been as therapeutic as it could be. So that route represented a lot.

What do you think the difference is between repeating a route and doing a first ascent?

Some people feel a sense of ownership in doing a first ascent, but for me it's not about that whatsoever. It's purely about exploration. I'll look at a boulder, and then all of a sudden I'll see a sequence. I like looking at rocks without chalk and trying to interpret where the path to the top would be. You can pick out one boulder amongst hundreds that has all the right qualities, and then clean it. And then for thousands of years, this one boulder will be

slightly cleaned. That's why I love it. I mean can you imagine what painters do? They look at a landscape, say, and they have an idea in their mind that's inspired by the landscape. Then they turn to a piece of blankness, and they create. For me, establishing routes is along the same lines. It's the most creative process in climbing, and you can share that experience with other people without you even being there.

What have you learned through the process of doing so many hard climbs?

When I look at things, I see more options, more possibilities. I think I can see things that will be done in the future, but I just don't know what it takes to do them. I can enjoy just hanging on a rope trying to project these things. Sometimes I'd like to hire Chris to drag around and say, "Try that move like this. Put your feet over here and see if it works." All I've learned is to have more imagination. I like thinking about what could be done, what's going to be possible.

Do have any other interests? What do you do when you're not climbing?

I read a lot. A lot of science fiction. I love learning different languages. I like to talk. I like to go places and see things. I like to see culture, society, cities, the world. I love, for example, taking a train to Italy and seeing all the old, bombed-out factories from the war, right next door to brand new buildings. I like to think, actually. I like to think out loud.

DAVE GRAHAM

One thing that you are known for is your level of motivation. Why do you think you're so motivated, and where do you think that comes from?

I don't know. I don't know at all, but I've always been like that and I always will. Some things you can't describe.

When you approach a hard route that you want to do, do you have a certain method that you always follow?

It's all about doing the moves, first of all. And once I do that, I start trying to climb it. Sometimes I'll spend hours or days just trying to do the individual moves. If I go up once and I can do all the moves, then I'll try it from the bottom. Sometimes, for example, I'll figure out one way to do something that I can do independently, but when I try and link it, it'll be too burly, so I'll have to figure out that section differently.

Do you follow a training routine?

I climb, and I exercise my mind as much as I can. I go to the gym every once in a while, if it's pouring rain. Or when I go out bouldering, I'll try and do specific kinds of problems that I want to work on. For example, one day I'll work on big burly moves, or crimps, or slabs. Or I'll decide to do one move at a time on a boulder. So I'll basically be practicing working a route, but without the rope. One of the biggest challenges, though, is finding a partner. I mean, I'd love to climb with Chris, for example, but he and I have

completely different lives and are completely different people. I think it's funny. I was really fascinated by and adored the idea of climbing with Chris, but we worked on it and it just didn't work out. It was hard.

When you have to give things a lot of tries, how do you stay motivated?

Bitching. I get pretty pissed off. I'll usually get really intense about my work routes.

Do you enjoy it when you fall off a lot?

Well, yeah. I like getting really angry through falling. It's not like I'm yelling, but I really put everything into it, and when I fall off, I have to regroup everything and start over again. And I have to figure out what I did or what I missed or why I wasn't trusting my feet. I think I just get really intense about routes and boulders because that's the kind of person I am. If I can't figure out how to say something, it will bother me equally as much. If I can't figure out how to explain something to somebody, it'll drive me crazy. It's the same way with routes, and I love it. I usually just have a high-energy session every time I climb, and it becomes more and more of a challenge. It's awesome. I get really into it. Trying to get from point *a* to point *b* is fascinating. But don't get me wrong; it's not all about literal joy. I mean sometimes you fall off something and feel like you're going to vomit because you just climbed 40 meters, and you really want to do it, but now you have to start over and try that hard all over again.

You said earlier that you were afraid of things. Does the fear not bother you when you want to do something? How do you deal with the fear when you really want to do something but you're afraid?

That's the only time I get really angry and frustrated. That's my big deal, when I get myself in a situation, and yet I still panic. On *Biographie,* for example, there's one spot where I always get my foot behind the rope. Every single time I get up there, I spend all this time kicking around and wasting all my energy. I just can't look at a rope behind my foot and then go for it. I can't. There's no chance. I'd rather skip a bolt than have my foot behind the rope. And that's what I mean. I get frustrated that I'm like that. It does, however, lead me to accept that I'm scared and recognize that I need to chill because I am. And it's not a big deal, because everybody does and should get scared. The only time I get really annoyed is when people won't give it to me. I'll be scared and won't want to do it, and I'm OK with that. I'll find another route, because that one just freaks me out. I want a break sometimes, and it bothers me when people won't give me a break. They expect something because of who I am or something.

What traits do you think have helped you to be successful?

I think the fact that I have a pretty positive energy. I mean it's rare that I make a whole crag miserable. I think I usually get people psyched, and that has gotten me really far

because then they reciprocate the feeling. Giving and receiving energy is massive to me. Maybe I give a lot of energy back into the climbing community; a lot of other people don't have that type of energy that extends like that.

How would you hope to be perceived by others?

I don't have any expectations of how they would perceive me. I've been perceived in so many radical ways. Maybe I would hope people would be open-minded, at least, and not judge me by my image that exists. There's nothing that's separating me from anybody, and I get tired of being isolated. Some people treat you differently because you rock climb better than they do. They treat you differently than they would otherwise. They treat you as a symbol of something rather than just another person. I would hope to be perceived as something other than just a good rock climber or the neurotic hyper guy. I don't think they even see me. I'm just Dave Graham, and that's not me, it's something that's been fabricated by American climbing magazines.

Are you ever not motivated?

For rock climbing? Yeah. But if I'm not motivated for that then I'm motivated for something else. I'm always psyched to do something.

Once he started climbing, nothing else mattered and the sport took over his life.

I first met Chris at the Junior Nationals

in San Diego, when all of us fourteen-year-old girls found ourselves with crushes on the incredibly strong, surfer-looking boy from Santa Cruz. Since that competition Chris and I have remained friends, as have many of our peers, despite intermittent contact. Growing up we often climbed together, traveled together, and competed together. Today Chris is no longer the gangly boy who was too strong and too young to realize that he needed to use his feet while climbing. He is a wise, thoughtful person and climber, whose body has morphed into the ideal climbing physique due to years of repetitive movement. Chris has big, knobby hands with swollen joints; massive forearms; and broad shoulders. His blue eyes stand out in contrast to his sun-bleached hair and tan skin, and his smile is wide and childlike, often turning into laughter when he is uncomfortable or unsure of the ideas he is trying to express.

Chris Sharma was born in April 1981 in Santa Cruz, California. He started climbing when he was twelve at a local gym called Pacific Edge. Previous to climbing he had spent a good portion of time climbing the unique trees that are abundant in Santa Cruz. Apparently something in him knew what he was meant to do. Once he started "real" climbing, though, nothing else mattered and the sport took over his life.

Chris excelled very quickly at climbing and soon began entering competitions. At fourteen, fresh from winning the Junior Nationals in San Diego, he and several peers decided to try their hand at the adult National Championships, held in San Francisco. Chris took first, and his friends also placed well, stunning the adult competitors. Clearly a new era within climbing was beginning. That same year, Chris became the youngest person in the world to climb 5.14c, a grade that even today is only climbed by the world's best climbers.

For Chris, though, this was just a beginning. He went on to excel in both indoor and outdoor climbing, setting records, creating standards, and breaking barriers. Though still very young he was soon a sponsored athlete, a "professional" climber, and unable to maintain both that lifestyle and the one of a high school student. Choosing climbing over "normal" life, Chris elected to receive an alternative diploma and pursue climbing full-time. He hasn't looked back since.

By the age of twenty, Chris was already an icon within the sport. Amazingly enough this kind of attention seems to have done little to affect his attitude or drive for climbing. He still climbs for the sheer love of the sport and eschews any mention of who is the best, saying that within the sport of climbing, such a label is completely beside the point.

When he was seventeen, Chris took a trip to France and landed at Ceuse, a climbing area with a stunning band of limestone capping a large hill outside the town of Gap. Ceuse, as is much of the climbing in Europe, is rife with climbing history. It was largely developed by one of France's own climbing icons, Patrick Edlinger. The cliff band holds some of the country's most classic and difficult climbs, including one that, at the time of Chris's arrival, was as yet unclimbed.

The climb was an extension of an already existing route called *Biographie,* rated 5.14c. Many of France's best climbers had tried it, but it refused to be conquered. During that trip Chris decided to give the route a try, but he was ultimately unsuccessful. Two years later, he returned to again try the still-unclimbed route. Again he was unable to do the route within the amount of time he had allotted himself. At twenty Chris returned yet again, and this time had his way with

Chris Sharma

Height: 6 feet

Weight: 165

Date of Birth: 4/23/81

Current Hometown: Santa Cruz, California

Age of First Climb: 12

Approximate Number of Days Per Year Spent Climbing: 222

Hardest Climb: *Realization,* Ceuse, France

Favorite Climbing Area: Mallorca, Spain

Chris refusing to let go,
Hampi, India

the 120-foot limestone route. He had fallen off the crux of the *Biographie* extension more than thirty times, each time taking enormous falls. His tenacity on the route, however, not only proved his talent, but also proved he had the ability to stick with it when success did not come as easily as he was accustomed to. Chris named the extension *Realization*, saying, "In French, to realize a route means to send it. Plus, it was very difficult for me mentally, emotionally, and physically, so in order to be ultimately successful, I had to 'realize' a lot of things about myself during the process." The climb was given the rating of 5.15a, a level that was previously thought to quite possibly be unreachable.

Aside from *Realization,* however, Chris's accomplishments stand at the pinnacle of several genres of the sport, including onsighting 5.14a; climbing and establishing numerous V15s and 5.14s; completing deepwater solo routes rated at 5.14, sometimes up to 80 feet above water; and winning competitions such as World Cups and the X Games.

So who is the person behind such amazing feats? Maybe not whom you'd expect.

The Interview...

How'd you end up going to the climbing gym?

I think I saw a video. We rented a movie called *K2* when I was a little kid, and I was fascinated. I don't know if you're predestined to things or if you have connections to certain types of things, but when I saw that movie, I just knew that was what I wanted to do. I didn't want to do anything else.

What about it fascinated you?

I was always climbing trees at that time, and climbing a tree when you're a kid is just fun. But when you see someone climbing in a movie, like an adult doing it, then it seems more real somehow, more legitimate. It was the grown-up version of something that I already liked doing. There were adults going out and getting serious about it, climbing on rocks. I think it made me realize that it could be taken to a much

CHRIS SHARMA

It just felt natural inside of me to climb. It felt ingrained in my being.

higher level or something. Plus, climbing just felt natural.

What about climbing felt natural?

Well, you're in a natural environment for one. But my mom would always talk to me about how I didn't crawl very much as a kid. And I guess crawling is really good for connecting your brain synapses, because when one foot moves, the opposite hand moves in unison. So she thought climbing was really good for me, because that's what you're doing on the wall. But really it just felt natural inside of me to climb. It felt ingrained in my being.

So the first time you went to the climbing gym, can you describe the feeling you had then?

I think I probably walked in and was just in awe. I thought it was the coolest thing I had ever done. Instantly. Like I was saying before, it was like climbing trees, but it was this official thing that you could do that was accepted as an activity or a sport. So when I went to the climbing gym and started climbing, for me I felt that I had found my passion. I remember the first time I went, my mom told me later that after trying it I said I wanted to be a professional rock climber. There was just a certain connection. I don't know why that stuff works or where those connections come from, but I guess it's just like you meet certain people and connect with them and others you don't.

Did you do any other sports before that?

I was always pretty athletic, but I never really focused on any particular sport. So when I found climbing . . . I loved it. I could do it by myself. The other team sports didn't really capture me like climbing did. Climbing is more of a loner sport I think.

How'd you start competing?

When you start climbing in the gym, it's just the natural progression, right? How do you go further than just climbing in the gym? You go to competitions. That's what was most available to me and how I started. It's what we did.

When did you start going outside?

I think the first time I went outside was probably a few months after I first started climbing. We went to Pinnacles National Monument and did an anchors course that the university offered.

When you started climbing, did you realize it was something you excelled at?

Well, it wasn't really in my mind. It was just something that I loved. I mean, people were telling me that I was getting good, and I was psyched to feel success. But it's weird. You never really know how "good" you are because it's a relative term. Things are always hard because you keep finding harder things to climb. And they're always

Communing with the natural world,
Santa Cruz, California

hard so you always feel inadequate. You never feel "good"—except when you do something. That's when it feels easy.

Was there anybody that was important to you as a climber or somebody that you looked up to or drew inspiration from?

I think I looked up to a lot of different people—mainly older people who took me under their wing. Guys I hung out with around Santa Cruz. My friends Andy, Sterling, and Chris Bloch. I met those guys and we started climbing outside, mostly at a place called Castle Rock. They were all older than me, like big brothers, and they just showed me the beauty of climbing outside and nature and this whole other side of climbing that's not just gyms and competitions. They showed me the value and importance of being outside with friends, having a good time, experiencing the rock, appreciating the natural creativity of nature. We would just go find new boulders, clean them off, and climb on them. And that experience gave me another way to look at and appreciate climbing that's not just performance alone. In climbing gyms it seems like it's all about performance and competitions—because that's really all there is to do—but when you go outdoors you learn how to appreciate the rock, the texture of it, the hold, how crazy it is that it's naturally like that. I feel like those guys taught me how to go out and see places to climb, find the line up the rock, find the problems—basically to have an imagination.

But also when we were in Hueco,

climbing with Marc (LeMenestrel). Remember that? That was totally inspiring for me. After that he definitely became a role model.

What was it about Marc?

I don't know. He just seemed completely genuine in spite of how amazing he was.

I still remember that day that we went climbing with Marc, even though it was like ten years ago. Seeing Marc climb was seeing someone who has obviously mastered a skill. In his case, climbing. And he just seemed really playful and like he was just having a good time out there with his friends. He wasn't too caught up in the whole game of climbing hard and trying to do the next hardest thing. It seemed like he was just doing it because he really truly loved it. And it was cool that he took the time to go climbing with us. He seemed really in tune with himself. I think that's what I got with him. Just to climb and enjoy it.

Did you ever make a decision to pursue professional climbing, or was it something that you feel you kinda fell into?

Well when I started doing all the competitions, it seemed like climbing was blowing up as more of a mainstream sport. I was having a lot of success, and I got to a certain point where I had to decide whether or not to pursue it—it was my dream, though, so there was really no decision. I found an alternative program for high school so I could pursue climbing, and that was when

I knew for sure that this was what I was doing. And I feel like I've learned a lot by getting to travel around the world and experience life. I'm happy with the choices that I've made.

Do you ever wonder or think about doing something else? What did you want to be when you were a kid?

I remember when I was a kid I wanted to be a ranger. Like a park ranger. Either that or a professional baseball player, I was thinkin'. But, you know, I started climbing when I was twelve, and that pretty much took me away from there. Everything else got thrown to the side.

How does it feel to know that wherever you go people expect you to be the best?

Well if I know it's going to be that way, then I can prepare for it, plan for it, or just accept it. But sometimes it's just very overwhelming. When it's just a couple of days, I can deal with it, I can put on a show or something, but some people are always constantly expecting to be amazed. I can't always satisfy that in people. It's not possible to always amaze people. You know sometimes I'm on and sometimes I'm off. On days that I'm off, hopefully people think it's cool to realize that I'm human, that I'm not on this other level that's untouchable from everybody else. But on the other hand, some people might be disappointed to realize that I'm not that special. People see me in videos and stuff and they get these ideas that I'm amazing. But then they see me and see that I'm just a normal dude. It might be a letdown, but I think it's good for people to see both sides of that, because so much of it is hype. So I just try to keep a positive attitude, whether or not I'm climbing my best.

Do you have bad days? And if so, how do you deal with them?

I definitely have bad days. Maybe sometimes I'll feel clumsy on the rock, or I won't feel coordinated, or I'll feel weak, like I can't pull. Or I'll just feel totally unmotivated. That's probably the leading cause of having a bad day. If I'm just feeling weak or clumsy, but I'm motivated, then it'll work itself out. But if I'm not really motivated . . . for example, if I'm climbing somewhere and there are some random strangers staring at me, and I'm not really in the mood to deal with that, then I'll get all uncomfortable and unmotivated and as a result I'll feel clumsy or weak. Sometimes I can't even climb. If I'm not motivated, it's hard to push past a certain pain tolerance.

So how do you deal with days like that?

It depends. If I'm not motivated and I don't want to climb, then I usually don't. But if I'm not climbing that well, it's OK with me. I don't mind going out and doing easy problems or routes just to move my body. I love doing that—just climbing a few notches below my maximum level. For me, doing that is often more fun. I really enjoy climbing things that I'm not maxing out on but are still hard enough that I'm forced to

CHRIS SHARMA

focus and use my body economically. Because when you're climbing at your maximum level, it's not really fun in the same way. It's more serious—you have to be very determined and willing to push past your pain tolerance. So sometimes it's nice to just go cruise and, whatever your level is, just bump it down a few levels. I love that. Just to have that feeling where you still have to be very present, but you can still enjoy it.

Have you ever gone through a time when you were just not psyched to climb at all?

Oh yeah. Totally. I've gone through times when I've wanted to quit. It's hard, because both of us have been climbing for so long. And it kinda becomes your identity, you know? You're a climber and you don't know anything else. And sometimes you want to escape that. You don't want to be stuck as just that. Especially when people think they know you and you have to deal with recognition.

Definitely at times I've really taken a step back. For sure when I hurt my knee. Before I hurt my knee, it was all la-dee-da. But then, like I was saying, you identify so strongly with being a climber, and when suddenly you can't climb you feel hopeless, totally lost. I think I went through that quite a bit when I was seventeen, eighteen, nineteen.

But actually I've kinda always been processing it. I'll get psyched, go climbing, then get turned off again for some reason. Every time though, I come back and feel stronger. I mean, my motivation for climbing feels stronger. And it just builds.

How do you feel about climbing now?

I'm just totally in my comfort zone. This is how I've directed all my energy, so I feel in my element. And it's good to be in your element to push yourself. Well, it's good to go out of your element to push yourself also. But I don't know, it just feels good to go climbing and be out in nature.

So it seems like success has come relatively easy to you, but when you did *Realization*, that was something that you initially failed at. How was that and how did you deal with it?

That whole process of climbing *Realization* was really draining. It was really emotional to get so worked up about one piece of rock. And it's so mental. You have to climb for so long, the crux is way up at the top, and the whole time you're kinda playing mind games with yourself.

There's so much stress about success. You just want to do it, so you're always thinking about getting to the top, and that distracts you—because you're not thinking about the present and flowing on the rock. I think it's really difficult to block the pressure of success out and stay focused on just climbing. That was a really cool experience, to try and get past that. It was awesome.

But it's also pretty full-on. Since then, all my climbing has been just going on little trips, bouldering, deepwater soloing, more just like being playful. Because it's so serious, the project thing.

And you didn't like that?

I liked it, but it required a lot of effort and time. It was just really intense and draining. It was a really cool process, and I loved it and I would be psyched to do it again, but it's so serious that it's hard to enjoy it all the time. When you're focusing on redpointing something, you can maybe only try it twice a day, and then you have to rest. You have to get all scientific, and sometimes it's more fun to just go climbing and discover things.

Right now, however, I'm totally ready for another project, because I haven't had anything that's really pushed me for a while.

Did you train for *Realization* in between attempts?

Of course I thought about it, but I didn't train for it. I would just get there, start trying it, and figure that since I was climbing this superlong route that's pretty hard every day, it would get me in shape.

Have you ever trained specifically for anything?

Sometimes when I know I'm going somewhere, I'll want to get strong, so I'll train a little bit, but it's more like body maintenance. Push-ups sometimes, or yoga, stretching. I never do pull-ups or anything. Once in a while I'll campus—by once in a while, I mean once every few years.

Over the years do you think you've developed any rituals, superstitions, or spiritual practices that have become a part of your climbing routine?

Maybe I have. I remember when I competed I would always visualize myself flowing through this tube. I would close my eyes and visualize swooshing through.

Do you still enjoy competing?

I think I've veered away a little bit, because I just really enjoy going climbing, exploring, finding new lines. That's the real deal for me. I don't really care who's the best. That seems totally beside the point. Plus you're climbing on artificial structures, and I'd rather climb the real stuff.

What do you think it is that has made you successful? Concentration, desire, fitness...?

There are so many different factors to being successful. Genetics for sure. And obviously being fit is important, because climbing is physical . . . but then there are all sorts of different factors. Some people are super strong, but have trouble putting it together on rock. I think it's important to be intuitive of your body and how it's interacting with the rock . . . and to have that desire, too. Climbing can be painful, so you gotta want it.

I think one of the hardest things for me these days is not having enough people around to push me. It's good to sometimes be in an atmosphere where people are supergood and pushing each other, and I haven't climbed like that in a while. I think it's really hard to one-up yourself, you know? It's easy to be competitive with

A young Chris on *La Rose et
La Vampire*, Buoux, France

someone else, but then to step it up a notch by yourself and push your own limit—it's hard to break that barrier and keep going. It's, well, it's easy to not push yourself once you feel like you're the best at something. It's easy to sit back and think that you're good enough. But to push through that and be your best, I think that's the hardest.

Who do you think has been there to push you in the past?

I think competition has provided that for me. It's helped inspire me to take it to the next level. Different climbers, as well, have pushed me; I'll see their level and try or want to go beyond that. But ultimately, like I said before, it's just about pushing yourself, finding your personal best—that is the most challenging thing. I mean, I've been climbing by myself for quite a while. Well, climbing in a group but with people who are a bit below my level—I feel like it sounds bad to say that—but, just as it's hard for someone to come climbing with me all the time because I want to try things that are harder, it's kinda the same way for me. I want to try things that are hard for me, but no one else wants to, so I end up trying them by myself. People will come and spot me sometimes, but they don't want to try the problems, so I just climb by myself mostly.

Have you thought of moving someplace where people might be there to push you?

I have thought a bit about relocating to different places around the world. I don't

know. I want to live someplace where there is climbing, because there's not so much climbing in Santa Cruz. I've been spoiled, though, growing up in Santa Cruz. It's perfect weather year-round, so it would be hard to beat. I'd like to find a nice place, nice temperature, maybe some ocean, some cliffs coming out of the ocean, some boulders . . . maybe the Mediterranean could be good.

Do you feel like you missed out on anything, having started climbing so young?

We make sacrifices and choices to do anything, and when we make certain choices we miss out on other things. But you gain something else. So no, I don't regret anything. I'm pretty psyched about where I am these days. You know if I didn't get into climbing, my path would be a lot different. I don't know what I'd be doing right now, that's for sure. I can't even imagine. Maybe I would have gone to college, I don't know.

How do you feel that climbing has affected or changed the person that you are?

Well, I've been climbing half my life, so it's a huge part of who I am and how I view the world. It's totally affected me. All the places I've been, where I've gone, who I've hung out with . . . everything.

CHRIS SHARMA

One of the things you seem to be known for is your spiritual approach to climbing. How would you define that part of your climbing?

I feel like when I go climbing . . . you have to be totally present. It's a very meditative thing to be so focused. I don't think I've ever been able to focus the way that I've been when I'm climbing. It totally channels my energy in such a way that I completely lose myself. And that is such a good feeling.

Do you consider yourself to be one specific religion?

No. I think I take things from wherever. I've studied quite a bit of Eastern philosophy—Buddhism and stuff—so that's kinda where I've taken my spiritual ideas from.

Do you think your parents have passed down their belief system?

Well, you know, I grew up in a bit of a different way. I grew up the way I grew up, and that has brought me to where I am. That's what all climbers have in common. We've all converged in this sport but have totally different backgrounds. We're from different parts of the world. But you meet all these people who have that common thread—climbing. It's pretty cool that we're all pretty impacted by something so fun.

How do you think your position within climbing has affected your relationships?

Well, it's brought me close to so many people. All my best friends and people I know are from climbing, so it's introduced me to so many people. It's been really positive in that sense, because the connections you make with people are pretty special. But then, for example, always being on the road traveling it's hard to have a girlfriend or to stay superclose to your family. So there are difficult things, too, but in order to be able to be there for other people, I think you also have to follow your own heart, too, and I feel like I'm following my heart by climbing. So I think that allows me to be there for other people. Maybe not always in the physical sense, but definitely emotionally and mentally, and I hope that the people I'm close to see that.

Do you have any dreams or goals for the future?

I'd be psyched to keep climbing. I'd also like to live somewhere. You know, I had a realization the other day. My parents got divorced when I was three, and I lived week on week off either at my mom's or dad's house for my whole childhood. And then by the time I was fourteen, we were going all around the world and stuff, so that's all I know. It's weird that it just occurred to me, but it's probably why I have this transient nature. It's a side of me that's always pretty comfortable to be on the go.

What has made you feel like you want to live somewhere recently?

I just want to be more stable. It's hard when you're on the road to have more of a life than just climbing. You can't focus on

anything else, because you're constantly moving and changing locations. If you live somewhere, though, then you can have your house, your little garden, your projects; you can take some classes; whatever. And then you could incorporate climbing into maybe a more normal life. Not normal, necessarily, but stable. Getting in touch with a place on a deeper level. It's hard to really get a feel for a place when you're just there for a week, two weeks, or a month. I don't know. I might get a van. That might be a good start.

Is there anything that you would want to express to a younger crowd?

I guess I would just want to encourage people to go climbing and learn from that. Being out in nature is such a powerful thing. I would encourage younger climbers to respect nature and ourselves, get to know our bodies, get in tune with the rock. Climbing is so fun and such a good experience, that I think it's important to not take it too seriously. It's not the end of the world—or the entire world either.

CHRIS SHARMA

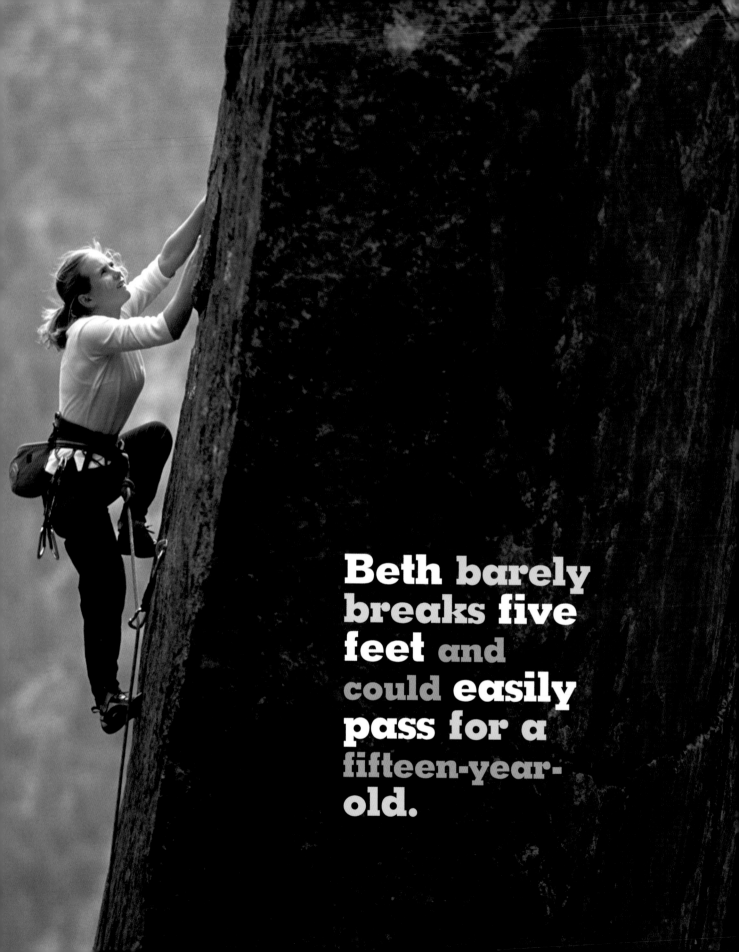

Beth barely breaks five feet and could **easily pass for a** fifteen-year-old.

Beth Rodden sits curled up in a chair

in the living room of her and husband Tommy Caldwell's 600-square-foot cabin in Estes Park, Colorado. In her hands she clutches an enormous mug of herbal tea. Beth barely breaks 5 feet and could easily pass for a fifteen-year-old. Even her hands are small and delicate, with long, slender fingers that look better made for piano playing than for shoving in thin cracks. Beth has thick, blonde hair and laughing blue eyes. When asked about anything other than herself, she is open and vibrant, but when asked about her own climbing, aspirations, and desires, she is somewhat reserved, choosing instead to remain a mystery. I wonder if her experience in Kyrgyzstan and the ensuing media rampage has had something to do with her reticence. Regardless, though, she has always been very private about her climbing "projects." Perhaps this secrecy frees her from living up to public expectations, and therefore allows her to truly push herself to her limit.

In 2000 Beth and three other climbers—Tommy Caldwell, John Dickey, and Jason Smith—were taken hostage by Islamic militants while on a climbing trip to Kyrgyzstan. They were held, without food and water, for six days. Their captives forced them to lie still in holes in the ground covered with branches and dirt during the day and to walk untold miles while under the cover of nightfall. They were finally able to escape, due to a heroic act on the part of Tommy, and ran nearly a dozen miles until finally finding friendly faces who escorted them to the American embassy. When the climbers first returned home, they were initially met with media fanfare, only to later have a reporter try to investigate and disprove their story. Anyone who knew these climbers, however, knew that the four people who returned from Kyrgyzstan were very different from the four people who had left. Beth, in particular, seems to have been profoundly changed and molded by her experiences in Kyrgyzstan. In some ways she seems years beyond her age, and in other ways she still seems to be the twenty-year-old girl who had her life interrupted in a country nearly halfway around the world.

Beth, originally from Davis, California, learned about climbing from her father, who had been an avid climber before her. As a child she had been climbing on several occasions, mostly outdoors in the Sierras, but it wasn't until she was nearly a teenager that she really took an interest in the sport. One day, instead of going to swim practice, she decided to hit up the climbing gym, and that decision ended up changing her life dramatically.

Beth had always enjoyed climbing, but it wasn't until she discovered the climbing gym that it became truly accessible to her, and she began riding her bicycle to climb almost every day after school. Before climbing, Beth had always been involved in sports, like swim team, where she had a coach and a strict practice schedule. Her personality turned out to be well suited to the freedom of climbing however, and she enjoyed being able to go whenever and do whatever she wanted.

Shortly after starting to climb at the gym, Beth decided to enter a local competition. She had a blast and ended up getting third in the recreational category. At the time, competitions were very popular, and everyone entered them, from little thirteen-year-old Beth, to the fifty-five-year-old retired businessman. There were several local, regional, and national competition circuits, and Beth decided after that first comp to enter the local circuit. She gradually worked her way up the ranks and before long found herself at the Junior Nationals in San Diego. Top competitors from that competition were all invited to Junior

Beth Rodden

Height: 5 feet, 1 inch

Weight: 108 pounds

Date of Birth: 5/30/80

Current Hometown: Estes Park, Colorado

Age of First Climb: 13

Approximate Number of Days Per Year Spent Climbing: 200

Hardest Climb: Number-wise— *The Optimist* (14b); Effort-wise—*The Nose*

Favorite Climbing Area: Yosemite

Beth letting loose at
Donner Summit, California

Worlds, in Laval, France, and Beth was one of those invited to compete against climbers her age from around the world. That competition in San Diego brought together a group of young climbers, including Chris Sharma, Tommy Caldwell, and others who were to change the face of climbing in the years to come.

Beth enjoyed competing and continued to pursue it for several years. She even became Junior National Champion at one point and was invited to the ESPN X Games on a couple of occasions. She mostly enjoyed the camaraderie of competitions and the fact that they gave her something to work toward when at home climbing in the gym. Within several years, though, she started meeting people who took her climbing outside, and she quickly discovered that she enjoyed climbing outdoors far more than indoors.

Throughout high school Beth continued to climb both indoors and outdoors, and after high school she enrolled in college at UC Davis. After just one semester, however, Beth was invited on an expedition to Madagascar, and it was that trip that truly changed her life's direction. After returning from Madagascar, Beth made the decision to take a semester off from school and spend her time in Smith Rock, Oregon. While there Beth became the youngest American female to climb 5.14a when she redpointed *To Bolt or Not To Be* after two months of work. This amazing accomplishment instantly gained her national and international recognition, and soon college was a distant memory, as more and more climbing became not only her career but also her life's focus and passion.

In the summer of 2000, Beth met Tommy Caldwell, and soon they were planning climbs together in Yosemite. Essentially Beth and Tommy started "dating" on El Cap while together attempting to free-climb the route *Lurking Fear,* on which they were ultimately successful. That route was the first of many routes together, and today they are two of the most accomplished climbers—both independently and as a team—in the world. Specifically, Beth is the first American female to establish 5.14b, with *The Optimist,* and in 2005 she completed a team free ascent of *The Nose* on El Cap with Tommy.

Beth is one of the most tenacious and goal-oriented climbers I have ever met. Tommy has said on several occasions that when Beth is psyched on something, she suddenly gets ten times better than when she is not psyched. Based on her list of accomplishments, many of which she has shared with Tommy, this statement must be true. Beth works hard, trains hard, and does not give up, and this mental tenacity is perhaps one of her most important strengths as a climber.

The Interview . . .

Why do you think you enjoyed climbing outside better than inside?

Well, this doesn't apply to everyone, obviously, but for me to be a good indoor climber, I felt like I had to train inside a lot, and I found that boring after four or five years straight. Plus, climbing outside means being outside. And you could grab any hold you wanted. I remember climbing an arête my first time out. There were some holds on the face to the right of the arête, and I kept asking if they were "on" the route.

How do you feel now about the years that you spent competing?

I'm glad I did it. I don't think I could be climbing as well as I am now if I didn't have that base. I mean, I'm glad that I'm not sitting in isolation still somewhere, but it was fun for a while.

I'm really **hard** on myself. **I definitely didn't feel** any pressure from my p●rents.

Did you ever feel pressure?

Yeah, but just from myself.

Are you hard on yourself?

Oh yeah. I'm really hard on myself. I definitely didn't feel pressure from my parents, and I wasn't really sponsored at the time, so I was pretty much just putting pressure on myself.

Did you ever reach a point where you made a conscious decision to pursue climbing, or did it just evolve?

I think it slowly evolved, but I think one of the turning points for me was going to Madagascar. I got to see Lynn Hill and Nancy Feagin, and how they got paid to go climbing and go on trips. I saw that they were doing it, and I thought that maybe I could make it happen. So after that trip I decided not to go back to school, for a while at least, and see how it was. You know, I didn't make much money at first— but luckily I have nice parents. Slowly, though, I started getting recognized and getting some raises. And then I met Tommy, my sugar daddy (laughs).

What was it about the lifestyle that Lynn and Nancy had that appealed to you?

That you could do what you wanted. I grew up with two parents who had a working job, went to college, and had everything lined out. So I liked how in climbing you could dictate your own schedule.

What accomplishment are you the most proud of?

Probably *Lurking Fear*, because I would probably have never tried that hard—except I was trying to impress Tommy. I probably never would have done that route. But I would think, "I really want Tommy to like me. Maybe he'll like me more if I lead this pitch."

It seems like one of your first big accomplishments was *To Bolt*. Why did you decide to try that?

Well, my thinking before that was that you could climb your hardest by onsighting. Because up until that point I had. And I'd always go up to Smith on school breaks, because it was one of the closest sport climbing areas. One spring break I had a really good trip, and I did some 5.13s. Well, people kept telling me that you could always climb one grade harder redpointing than you could onsighting. I didn't really believe them, but I had a friend who was telling me I should try *To Bolt*, so that comment stuck in my head. I did try it once that trip, but I thought it seemed ridiculous.

After that trip, though, I got it in my head. So when I took a semester off of school, I decided to go up there to try it. And I had such a great time up there. I got to hang out with Brittany Griffith and Jim Karn, so I didn't really want to leave, and I was slowly making progress on *To Bolt*, so I just stuck it out.

Did you think you'd be able to do it at the outset?

When I first got on it, I thought no way. I could hardly do any of the moves . . . well, I could do some of the moves. But anyway, I just kept trying it and slowly got a little better and a little better, and then all of a sudden I was redpointing it.

What's the emotional or mental process that you go through when you're trying to redpoint a route?

I think maybe I'm just stubborn. I don't want to give up on something until I know that it's impossible. My thinking is that if you keep seeing progress—not even every day, but every few days—then you have something to work with. I'll think, "OK, when is the progress going to stop?" And then eventually maybe it doesn't stop, and then you do it. And if it does stop, then maybe it's impossible. I also like having something to work on because it gives me focus. If I don't have something to work on, then I just feel scattered. I'll be like, "Should I go climbing today? Naaa, maybe not." And then I end up never climbing.

How did it feel to do that route?

I was psyched to do it. It was a huge leap for me. I think I climbed 13a or b before that, so I was really excited. I never thought I would climb 5.14 after that, ever again.

Why not? After you've done it once you can do it twice, right?

Yeah, but I always thought that I was only good at these crimpy, low-angle routes, and I figured that there was nothing in the world like *To Bolt*. I thought, "This is it. It's all downhill from here." Hence the reason I took up trad climbing. I had many different ways to improve there.

And what was the deal you made with Jim Karn if you did the route?

I had to get drunk. And I got drunk. I had a big welt on my forehead.

And have you been drunk since?

No, much to Jim's chagrin. He's always wanting to make other deals with me, like, so, for example, he'll ask, "How about if you lead *Overboard* today you get drunk?" It's a 5.11 warm-up at Smith!

So what is it about Yosemite that draws you there?

Well, at first I would just go there to boulder with the guys from the gym in Davis. At the time I'd see people on El Cap and think that I would never do that, because it looked really scary. But then I went there one time to try and climb a wall before I went to Madagascar—I had no wall-climbing experience—but we didn't end up climbing one. After Madagascar, though, I thought, "Maybe I could get good at this trad thing." I thought that it might help me become a better climber, plus it opens more doors. You have more options, more possibilities for things to do and places to go. So I went down there one fall by myself

Beth making her way to the chains during her onsight of
The Phoenix **(5.13a), Yosemite National Park, California**

and hooked up with the locals—mainly this one guy named Ben—a really nice guy. And I had a ton of fun. We just climbed the classics, but I loved it. The next spring I went back, and that's when I climbed with Tommy. And I kept going back, because things are a lot easier when you always have someone to put up a toprope for you.

Do you realize I'm recording this?

I am the toprope queen. People can know that I'm a toproper.

Why *Lurking Fear*?

Brittany Griffith actually thought of it. I had planned to go to Yosemite and try it with her, but then I think she had to go somewhere else. So, just like on *To Bolt*, I then had it in my head. It's almost as if once somebody mentions it I can't get it out of my head.

But anyway, I couldn't find anybody to climb with, and Tommy ended up having no partner either, so . . . gosh darn it, I hate when that happens (laughs). I suggested that we try *Lurking Fear*, and that was it. We just plucked away at it.

Tell me a bit about *The Optimist*.

I think I had heard about it. People were always saying that there was a project in Smith that would be good if you had small fingers. And of course I thought, "I have small fingers."

BETH RODDEN

Was there something about the fact that nobody had done it? Did that appeal to you?

Yeah, that appealed to me in some regard, but I also think that just trying to climb my hardest appealed to me as well. We went to Smith one time when I was still in my foot cast, and I jugged up it and felt the holds. Then Tommy got on it, tried it a little bit, and thought it might go. By the time my foot healed, it was too hot in Yosemite, so I thought we could go to Smith and try that. And I just got into that same stubborn pattern. I spent a lot of time on it, and I really wanted to do it if I could, so I wanted to stay until I knew whether or not I'd be able to.

Did you realize that it would be groundbreaking?

No. Not at all. I can't really put a number on it, but I did not think it was going to be that hard at all. No way.

Is there a difference between doing an FA and redpointing a route?

There's a sense of satisfaction in putting up an FA, even if it's a 5.10. We were just in Norway, putting up 5.10s, and it was an amazing feeling to realize that nobody had done these routes before, nobody had touched that rock or seen the views that we saw, but now they'd be able to. It was really cool. But also, just climbing that hard too, it was incredible to me that I could push myself that hard.

Do you think you might be able to push yourself harder now?

No . . . no. That was good. I'm done.

Why'd you name it *The Optimist*?

Because I'm a pessimist, and Josh (Lowell, filmmaker) said I should name it *The Optimist,* to be satirical. The entire time

More Climbers to Watch

Daniel Woods

Date of Birth: 8/18/89

Years Climbing: 11

Hometown: Longmont, Colorado

Known For: Quick ascents of some of America's hardest sport climbs and boulder problems (up to V14/5.14c) at a very young age

Cruising on *The Sphinx Crack*
(5.13), South Platte, Colorado

I was working the route I kept saying, "I'm never going to do this. I suck. If only I was stronger." And then one day, under my breath, and forgetting that I was wearing a microphone and that Josh was listening to me, I did a move and I said, "Oh. That was good. Maybe that would help and I could do it." So of course Josh was like, "Ha."

Have you ever felt burned out or wanted to do something different with your life?

Yes. After Kyrgyzstan for sure. There was basically a nine-month period where I didn't want to have anything to do with climbing, but I made myself go, and I'd only climb a half-hour or so in the gym. And then there was a three-month period where I didn't climb at all. But at that time I think my feelings toward climbing had a lot to do with all the emotional stuff that I was trying to sort through. As for actual burnout, I think I've learned how to notice that and just take time off and not push myself.

How do you think Kyrgyzstan changed who you are as a person?

I think it made me grow up a lot. I feel like it made me see the big picture. It definitely made me appreciate friends and family a lot more. It's made me realize that I need to not take them for granted. But on the downside, it probably has also made me a lot more paranoid.

And how do you think it changed

your approach to climbing? Why didn't you want to climb when you got back?

I just didn't find joy in climbing after I got back, at all. But I kept making myself go, because that's what I did. It was my "job." I thought maybe if I didn't want to climb, I should go back to school, but I didn't really have any desire to do that, so I just didn't know what to do. And I got paid a little bit of money to climb, and when I did like it, I was halfway good at it, so I thought maybe I should keep doing it and hope that things changed.

How do you think that experience has changed how you view climbing?

It's hard to put into words. It may sound a little corny, but I think that I enjoy climbing more. I think I "take it all in more," as cliché as it sounds. For example, when we were on *Lurking Fear* I knew that it was beautiful, but I was also thinking about whether or not I could redpoint the next pitch or whatever. But now I feel like I *really* notice things, like how ridiculously beautiful it is twenty pitches up on El Cap, or how amazing it is that I get to go climbing every day. I feel like I appreciate it more.

Is there anything in your past that you wish you had done differently?

Yeah, I'm sure. Tons, but . . . I wish I wasn't so naive. I don't know. That's a hard

But now **I feel like I** really **notice things,** like how **beautiful** it is . . . **or how amazing it is that I get** I go **climbing every day.**

question. I mean, sure I have plenty of regrets. I regret not finishing college.

Why's that?

Because I think it's good to be educated. I'd like to go back maybe, when I know what I want to study.

Do you think that your lifestyle has provided you a certain amount of education though?

Oh yeah. I don't regret choosing the life I did, because there's no way I would have done all that I have. So, I don't regret it in one way, but I do in another.

Is what you like about climbing now different from what you liked when you first started climbing?

I probably appreciate the traveling more now. I realize how special it is and how not everyone gets to do it.

Why is it that you like tackling such big projects?

Probably just because it's a way to push myself.

Why do you think you and Tommy work so well together?

I honestly think it's because we care more about the other person than we do about ourselves.

What do you think are some of your strengths and weaknesses as a climber?

My strengths are probably slab climbing and standing on my feet. My weaknesses are anything powerful where you actually have to pull on your arms.

Do you think you'll climb forever?

As long as my body will let me. I'd like to.

How do you think being in the spotlight has affected you?

Well, it's definitely made me not want to go climbing in crowded areas, because I feel like I'm on display. I always imagine people are thinking, "Oh my gawd, she just fell on a 5.10. I should get paid to go climbing." But I also think that—I mean, it's what has allowed me to do what I do. If you couldn't get paid to go climbing, then I wouldn't be able to do it full-time.

How would you hope to be perceived by others?

How I truly am—shy.

You're not shy!

I am around people I don't know! I guess I'd just hope to be seen as genuine.

How do you think people perceive you?

As a ten-year-old. Just kidding. I don't know; I try not to think about it.

Beth redpointing *Sarchasm* (5.14a), the highest 5.14 in the U.S. at 11,500 feet, Rocky Mountain National Park, Colorado

What are you afraid of?

People with guns. Falling. Leading. Highballs. Spiders.

What is one thing that people would find surprising about you?

That I don't like to lead. Actually, you know, we've been doing a lot of slideshows and climbing festivals lately, and one thing that people keep saying to us is, "I can't believe how real you guys are." I think because we'll go bouldering with them, and I'll fall on a V4 and not throw a hissy fit or whatever. But we're just people.

Is there anyone that you look up to?

Tommy, for one. And you might say this is really corny, but for a long time, you.

Why me?

Because back when we were competing together, you just seemed to be so at ease with it all. I felt like you had it figured out. And you didn't really care about publicity. You just went out there and crushed everybody, but then were really humble about it.

Why do you think *The Nose* hasn't been repeated before now? What sets it apart?

First off, I don't think it's been repeated because it's just plain hard. Perhaps people saw how easily Lynn dispensed with it and expected it to be easier, but when it wasn't, got discouraged. Also it's basically the most famous rock climb in the world, so it's really crowded, making it that much harder, logistically, to work on. I know we backed away from it for several years because of the crowds. This year, though, we just decided to work with the crowds. And because it is so famous, it seems that every ascent of *The Nose* (first ascent, first one-day ascent, first free ascent) has marked a historic milestone in climbing, where other routes are not necessarily that way. All in all it's a very daunting route to try and free-climb.

What was the most challenging part for you?

As an individual pitch, the Changing Corners pitch. It's *really* hard and forced us to climb in ways that I never would have considered possible—hip scumming, arm scumming, etcetera. As a route, I think that learning to push my body to a new tolerance of stamina and suffering was a huge challenge. My feet were in so much pain that I thought a few times I would have to give up.

What was the most challenging part for you as a team?

For me, I fought the fact that I delayed Tommy for a couple of weeks. He was ready to go for the redpoint before me, and I knew that he was waiting for me, so I wanted to be able to do it sooner. But doing it as a team was so much more rewarding than we ever could have imagined.

Have you thought about trying to do it yourself in a day?

I think that I did it in the best style I can think of. Most people would probably think that doing it by myself would be better, but the challenge of team logistics is difficult and adds another step. Not being able to have someone jug with all your stuff, etcetera. I'm psyched with how I did it, and that I got to share the accomplishment with someone. As for doing it in a day, I don't think my feet could handle that right now, and I don't know if I could climb fast enough.

How did it feel to repeat such a historical route?

Superpsyched!

Do you see yourself as a role model for younger women who are climbing? How would you want to influence the younger generation?

To go out and pursue your goals and dreams. I think it's a pretty cool life if you can make it happen, so you might as well try.

BETH RODDEN

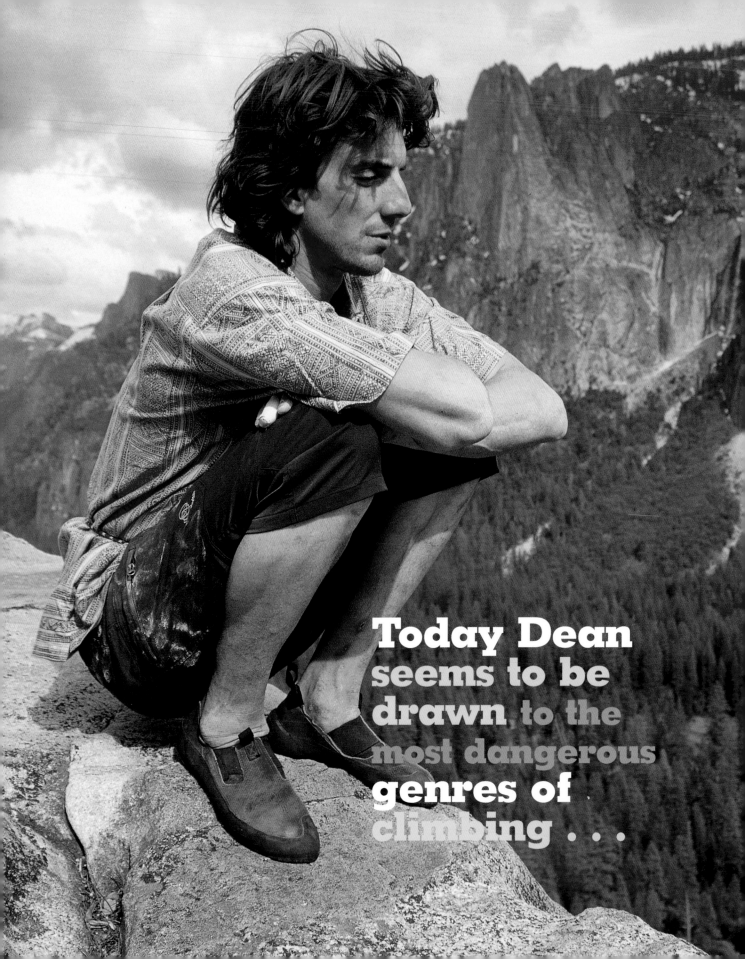

Today Dean seems to be drawn to the most dangerous genres of climbing . . .

Dean Potter is well over 6 feet tall, with a wild mane of dark hair, wide-set eyes, and a big smile. As a child Dean lived with his family in Israel. He tells me that he was afraid of heights and yet somehow still drawn to climbing on the stone house where he lived. After falling off the house and getting a concussion, Dean relates that his fear of heights was gone. Today Dean seems to be drawn to the most dangerous genres of climbing, including free soloing, highlining, and BASE jumping. He has a very esoteric approach to climbing, and his views about why he is drawn to these activities include accessing other senses, achieving a hyper-state of awareness, and focusing a mind that is constantly whirring.

Dean himself seems to be a mysterious man. Upon first meeting him, he seems quiet and distant but with an almost frenetic energy glinting out of his eyes. Once talking, though, he is friendly and open. Perhaps the former part of his personality is what has led him to climb so often by himself. This ability to push himself with no partner or support team has led him to accomplish incredible feats, including soloing or free soloing three of the hardest peaks in Patagonia—*Supercanaleta* on Fitzroy, *Compressor Route* on Cerro Torre, and the *Californian Roulette,* also on Fitzroy.

Dean may have been first introduced to climbing as a five-year-old in Israel, but it wasn't until his Army father retired in New Hampshire that he truly had the opportunity to explore climbing. The family lived near a cliff called Joe English, which was incidentally on an air force base. Being a typical teenager, Dean decided it would be "cool" to break in, and once in discovered a 200-foot cliff that drew him back again and again. Without the benefit of ropes, gear, or climbing shoes, Dean and a couple of friends began scrambling around the cliff in their Converse sneakers. Dean's career as a free soloist had already begun. He was sixteen.

Soon Dean's parents discovered what he was doing and forbade him to go, but between his desire to climb and pure teenage rebelliousness, there was no stopping him. It wasn't until a year after first discovering Joe English that Dean ran into other climbers who offered to teach him a safer way to pursue the sport. Soon he and his friends learned how to use ropes. They set up topropes and then truly began to test their mettle on the cliffs.

Soon, though, Dean graduated high school and headed for college, during which his climbing was put on hold. He attended the University of New Hampshire and joined the rowing team. According to Dean, college was "partying, learning how to live on my own, and rowing." This lasted for only a year and a half, however. Dean relates that he was very competitive and had a very competitive rowing coach. "He taught us that you didn't just beat the competition, you humiliated them. Even with my teammates I felt like I wanted to destroy them." The feeling of competitiveness controlled Dean—but then he went climbing after a year and a half off. He recognized that feeling of competitiveness as something he had never felt with climbing, and that day of climbing changed the course of his life forever. The next day Dean drove back to school, dropped out, and quit the rowing team. It was a decision that he has never once regretted.

The Interview....

What kind of climbing were you drawn to the most?

I liked to solo. After I quit school, I moved to North Conway and lived within a quarter mile of two amazing climbing areas—Cathedral and White Horse. I would go to one of those two areas nearly every day and solo.

Why were you drawn to that kind of climbing?

I could get away from everything. My brain is always grinding away at some problem or something. When I initially quit school and moved, I wondered if I was doing the right thing. But every time I'd go climbing, all my thoughts would vanish and I'd be superhappy. And it was even more magnified if it was just me—not even the distraction of another person there. It was the best thing that I had going, and it felt the

DEAN POTTER

best, and luckily I trusted those feelings.

Also it wasn't until I started climbing that I really had close friends, so that was another thing that made climbing special to me. I finally found a group of people that I belonged to, and that was a huge deal for me.

I read that you spent a fair amount of time in Hueco. What was Hueco like back then?

I went there in 1992, and it was my first road trip. I left New Hampshire with $350, went to Colorado, then to Wyoming. I went because all the climbers had left

Dean Potter

Height: 6 feet, 5 inches

Weight: 195 pounds

Date of Birth: 4/14/72

Current Hometown: Yosemite, California

Age of First Climb: 5

Approximate Number of Days Per Year Spent Climbing: Every day, at least in my mind

Hardest Climb: Out of the mainstream

Favorite Climbing Area: Wherever I am

New Hampshire, it seemed. There had been a really good scene, always people to climb with, but all of a sudden everyone left and moved to Colorado or Wyoming. I didn't have hardly any money, but it was getting pretty boring in North Conway without anyone to climb with, so me and this other guy left, drove this beater car out, and tried to get odd jobs. The worst job was on an assembly line working for a golf manufacturer.

I made a few hundred extra dollars and from there went to Hueco. And that winter I met all these guys who are still some of my best friends. There weren't too many people bouldering back then at Hueco, and a lot of us had hardly any money. Some of us even went on food stamps for a while.

One winter there were several climbers who came to Hueco and really impacted us. We thought we were climbing pretty hard back then, you know, V10. That was as hard as Hueco was, so we thought we were great. But then Fred Nicole and Elie Chevieux and Jacky Goodoff all came and pretty much flashed all of our hardest problems. We were super blown away by that. Mostly with Elie—he inspired us the most because he didn't look strong, but he would climb amazingly, and it didn't look like he used much power. For example, we saw that we couldn't be like Fred, because he was too strong. So Elie was kinda who I wanted to climb like—although I still don't. Then a year or so later, Marc LeMenestrel came to Hueco, and he was really beautiful to watch. He was a huge influence on all of us. He wasn't so into the numbers and would pick problems that looked beautiful rather than problems that were just difficult.

Dean free-soloing on the thirtieth pitch of *Freerider*, El Capitan, Yosemite National Park, California

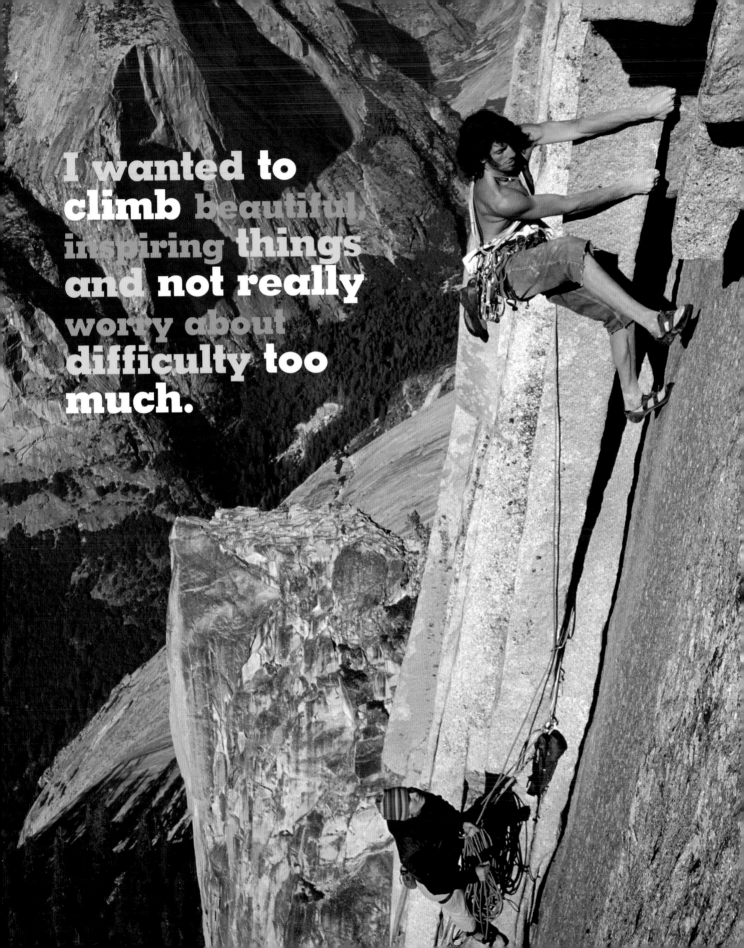

I wanted to climb beautiful, inspiring things and not really worry about difficulty too much.

After climbing with those guys, I started to consolidate my views on climbing and what I wanted to strive for. I wanted to climb beautiful things and inspiring things and not really worry about difficulty too much. I started feeling that way very strongly, so after that climbing mostly represented trying to do the things about which I felt the most passionate and that looked the most beautiful.

How'd you make the transition from that to climbing as a career?

A lot of my friends still tease me about that. Some people were sponsored back then, and it was weird for all of us. I think a lot of us were a little jealous, but instead of saying, "Man, I'm jealous," we would say that being sponsored was stupid. And also I saw that it wasn't so much who was the best climber, it was more about how much you worked it. I didn't really like that and I didn't want to be a part of that, so I never really pursued it.

But then I went to Yosemite with a friend of mine, Rolo, and started to climb there. And I really flailed around at first. I wasn't supergood at it, but I really liked it, so I just kept plugging away. I had huge epics trying to climb the big faces in a day. I didn't know much about big wall climbing and wasn't at all ready for what I was doing, but I'd still try them in a day. Finally, though, I started to know what I was doing, and then I just started climbing things in a way—free soloing or speed soloing—that was different and that no one else was really doing. I had no association with

any companies, but then a couple of companies called me up and asked me if I would work with them. At the time I was washing windows in Yosemite and had a pretty awesome life there. I was making one hundred bucks a week and didn't really think about anything but climbing. I guess I had kinda ragged on people who were sponsored athletes, but it just seemed like I had to do something to survive. So I kinda hypocritically said "Yeah, why not?" But I did feel a little different, because I never asked for it. And I guess that's the way I made it feel OK. It just felt stupid to say no to something free. And that helped me start climbing more all the time and going on trips.

So how'd you get into alpine climbing?

Pretty early on I moved to Estes Park to climb on the Diamond. One day a friend and I were climbing the *Yellow Wall,* and that was when I met Steph. I was pretty much superattracted to her early on. The *Yellow Wall* was one of the more amazing climbs I had ever done, and it's pretty much alpine climbing, which I hadn't done much of, so it felt really scary to me. But that was what I always liked the best— being out of my comfort zone. So anyway, after climbing I met back up with Steph and asked her out. So we made plans to come back the next weekend and climb the Diamond together. That was kinda how alpine climbing happened. Because I wanted to go out with Steph (laughs). Not really . . .

How does alpine climbing compare to rock climbing?

I think I almost like bouldering the best, because it's so chill, but for some reason I feel most drawn to climb alpine faces. In the same way I can't really explain why I like soloing things. It feels super-uncomfortable, but I'm always drawn back to wanting to be in the mountains alone. I think that's where I really discover who I am and what's inside me. So I guess it's just the searching side of me that likes alpine climbing. When I go alpine climbing, I feel like I come away with a few more answers to what I'm about. For example, I see that a more simple way of living makes me happy. A warm sleeping bag, a nice pad, not being soaking wet, something warm to drink—it's about as good as it gets. And I sometimes forget that when I'm just living a normal life. Plus I think that alpine climbing really scares me, and I don't want to be bound by my fear. If I'm afraid of something, then I'm drawn to it because I don't want to let it rule me.

Is that why you are drawn to climbs or forms of climbing that are life or death?

That's one of the reasons for sure. Another reason is that my mind is always wandering. I have a hard time focusing, but when I'm in a really dangerous or intense situation, I find that I have a superclear focus. And sometimes just to be able to have that feeling of clarity makes me feel good enough that it's worth the risk.

Do you think you thrive on that level of danger then?

It's more of where it brings me. For some reason when I'm soloing or doing more intense things, that's the only way I can really be focused. I've always been into mystical things, intuition, and other senses, and I think those really tune in when you're in a dangerous situation. You know how sometimes without even talking you just know what other people are thinking? If I'm in a life-or-death situation, it seems like I have more senses than just tasting or seeing or feeling. I tap into things that are usually only there randomly. There are all these random things that happen in life, like you know your friend's going to call before they do, or something like that. And when I'm soloing, I feel like I know things are going to happen before they happen. I feel really tuned into how I feel. I feel real connected to the world and myself. And all those feelings are the best feelings I know, so that's why I'm drawn to the danger of things, because it puts me in this super-aware state.

When have you been the most scared?

I was BASE jumping into a cave in Mexico, and I had a terrible parachute malfunction. The chute wouldn't open, so I was about to slam against the wall of the cave. If that happened, I probably would have died. I gained control of my parachute at the last second, though, and turned away from the wall but hit a rigging rope that's right there. I grabbed the rigging rope, and by that time my parachute had opened but

Speed-soloing on *The Nose*, El Capitan,
Yosemite National Park, California

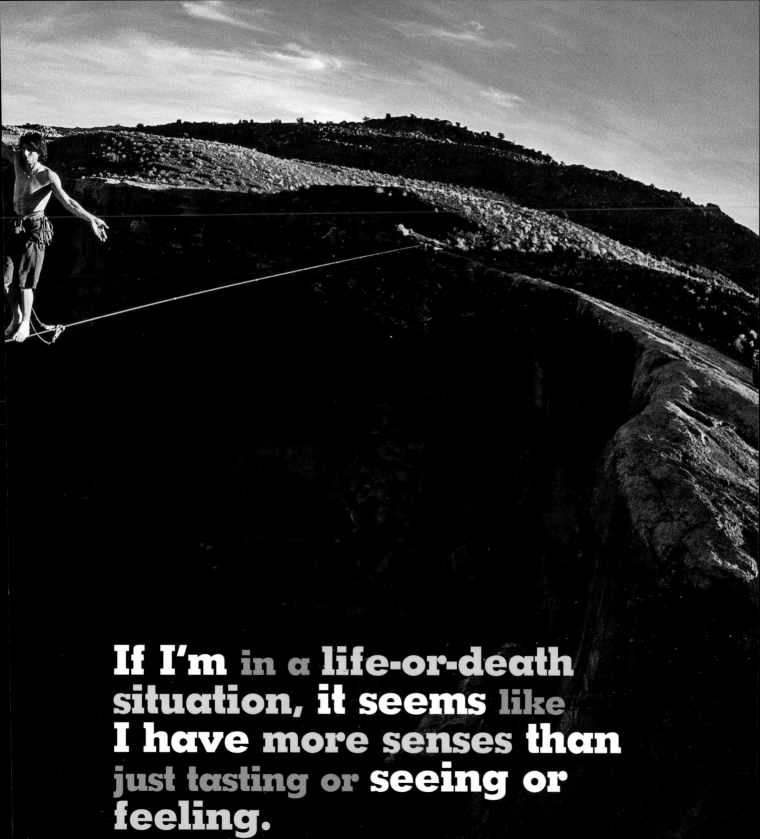

If I'm in a life-or-death situation, it seems like I have more senses than just tasting or seeing or feeling.

wasn't working. It flopped onto my head and kinda blinded me. I held onto this rope for 300 feet as I zipped down it. And this was all over the course of a couple of seconds. I think the most scared I've been is when I first latched onto the rope. I could feel that I was just a few seconds from hitting the floor of the cave from 300 feet.

How do the kinds of climbing that you pursue affect your relationships?

I think that maybe I'm too intense of a person for a lot of people. For the people that can deal with me, though, I try to show them that I love them. I really value this moment and the time that I'm alive, and I think it makes me more straightforward and truthful—I try not to leave anything unsaid. I want to live a proud life, where I know I didn't lie, I was as good to everybody that I could be, and—kind of on a superstitious level—I don't want to have bad karma. So it kinda makes me live better and try to be a better person.

Why did you decide to do those routes in Patagonia on your own?

Everything I look at I want to free solo. Fitzroy is enormous, and the fact that I could free solo it at all was really compelling. *Californian Roulette* had never been free soloed, and that pushes me a little bit, breaking new ground. That, in addition to a 6,000- or 7,000-foot alpine climb that I could climb free solo. Well that's as good as it gets to a guy like me. It was sort of the

same for the other routes. I wanted to free solo Fitzroy, and the easiest route was the *Supercanaleta.*

There are times in my life when I will want to do something so bad. I don't want to die or anything, but I don't want to live and not do it. It's too much for me. And Fitzroy was like that. I felt totally drawn with everything in me. I remember sleeping at the base of the route and feeling closer to myself and closer to that mountain than I ever have to anything. I just had all these really good feelings and was really happy. I think it's a common misconception that you have to be in a sad place to want to solo, but for me I feel really happy and alive and I want to do the climb with everything that I have. Also I had to wake up at two in the morning to do the route, and normally I have a hard time waking up, but boom, I just woke up and felt totally alert and happy, and it just seemed like every little bit of me wanted to do it.

Which one of the three did you feel was the most difficult?

Californian Roulette. It was the third one I did, and it had been tried by people a bunch. Some people had made it pretty far, but never summited. Also there was a lot of fear involved, because there was this big serrac that you have to climb under for about 5,000 feet. It's huge, and it groans the whole time you're climbing under it, and it could fall down basically anytime. Also it's ancient, ancient ice, so you can't even get your tools into it. The only way to get past the serrac is to climb this smear of vertical ice that's only 3 to 6 inches thick, for 150 feet. That smear is what makes the

Dean, Steph Davis, and Fletcher
in El Capitan Meadow

whole route possible. So I knew I had to go through that, but it's pretty intimidating to be right next to this big cave of ice that wants to fall on you and is kind of groaning. Also I'm not that good of an ice climber, and that smear was as hard of an ice pitch as I'd ever led and I was soloing. I remember being so afraid under the serrac that for 5,000 feet I was pushing harder than I probably should have, and it took

quite a while for my heart to stop racing. At that point the route joins an aid route, so I was free soloing through pitches that had only been aided before.

Also about two weeks before, this friend of mine had died on the route, so I was basically following him, and I could see the last signs of him. And actually he hadn't been found at that point, so that was partly what made me do the route. I

DEAN POTTER

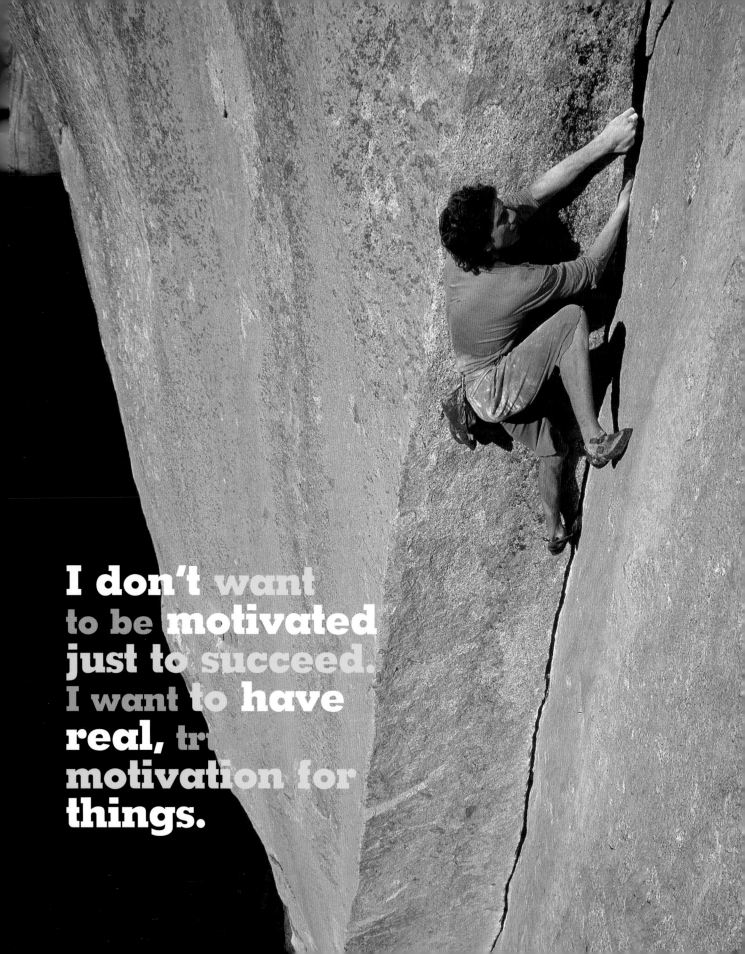

I don't want to be motivated just to succeed. I want to have real, tr... **motivation for things.**

had hoped that maybe I would find him or figure out what had happened to him. The whole experience was like nothing else.

Why do you think that route had been unsuccessful?

Mostly because everybody had been trying it in the traditional style, and that takes too long. The weather windows aren't long enough. Also, in my opinion, it had just gotten a bad reputation because people had died on it over the years. People had seen the serrac go and just demolish everything, so it had actually only been tried a couple of times. It wasn't like it was being tried every year. It was just really scary looking, so to me it was a real obvious way to go.

So, back to Yosemite. Are you now trying to do Half Dome, El Cap and Watkins in a day?

Mm-hmm. I've been flailing pretty hard on it.

How long did it take you to do just Half Dome and El Cap?

It took me twenty-three hours.

So having to add another whole mountain . . .

Yeah. And Watkins is the hardest of the three climbs.

Oh really?

The *Warren Harding* route, the south face. It took me a while just to do the FFA of that. That was a pretty big thing for me. And

then to try and do it in a day, just the one route was kind of a big deal. So I've tried twice to do all three in a day and failed both times on the crux of Watkins. It's a real slippery climb. The crux is probably 5.13, and it's at pitch forty, so I have to do 5.13 slab moves when my feet are very tired and sore. I came really close once, but it feels much harder than it does normally. I've been trying to increase my free-climbing ability so that it won't feel like a maximum pitch, but that's always been the hardest thing for me to do. This is the longest that I've flailed trying to do something, but I do think that trying it has been some of the best that I've climbed.

I'm getting to the point, though, where I'm kinda having these motivation questions. I don't want to be motivated just to succeed. I want to have real, true motivation for things. But sometimes, lately, I think I've allowed motivations like publicity and stuff to enter into my mind too much. So I'm trying to pull back from that, and as I've done that I've found a little loss of motivation. Things that used to inspire me—being a little competitive or breaking new ground—I'm beginning to see this little negative side in doing that. I feel like there's too much ego in that. And where it used to push me, now I think it's bad and it lessens my motivation. So probably in the last year or so, I've been having this struggle with what is OK to feel when I climb. When I was first climbing, I didn't feel that I wanted to be first or to be the best. I'd much rather be the way I was when I was a kid than an egomaniac. There's too much of that in our world. Trying to be first, trying to be the best, trying to be the strongest. I don't want my climbing to be like that.

Do you consider yourself a competitive person?

I think I have that pull in me, but it's getting less and less, and now when I feel it I try to go the opposite direction. My friends think it's OK to be competitive, because it can push you forward in a good way. But I think maybe I'm too competitive or something, so I try to let the feeling go away and not allow it to rule me.

Can you tell me a bit about the highwire that you did in Yosemite?

Yeah. I've been pretty into slacklining, and I started learning a lot about historical tightrope walkers. People have been walking tightropes for about 3,000 years, and it's kind of traditional to walk unprotected. Also, the most beautiful experiences I've had climbing are when everything is simplified. So, to me, free soloing is the simplest thing, until you learn to fly or walk on air—which I feel is all possible. And then free-solo slacklining or highlining is one of the most intense things I've ever done. It pushes me to that hyperaware state.

Can you describe the experience?

I feel that you just have to trust the things you're drawn to. It seems super-unnatural to want to go out on that line without any protection. You know, if you fall and don't grab the line, it's over. So until I get into a

certain groove, my mind and body are rebelling. I feel nauseous and dizzy, and everything in me wants to turn around. But my mind wants it—more than anything. So it's really empowering for me to be able to tell myself to do something and then make it happen. But then also, when I do push through, it's the gateway to all these extrasensory senses that I don't normally have. The first few times I walked leashless, I would just focus on the other side and see nothing else. But now it seems like it opens me up to everything. If people have been there, I'll know what's going on with them a little bit. I'll hear really clearly and see really clearly. Every bit of me is just superalert, and every cell of my body is focusing.

How do you think climbing has changed since you started?

I think that it's still coming along in lots of ways. I think people are more accepting of each other. There are still people who say that their way is the only way, but it seems that climbers are more accepting of what others do and not saying bad things about one another as much. Also it seems that people think anything can be climbed now, and I think that climbers' vision of what was possible used to be more limited.

Where do you see climbing going in the future?

I'd like to see it go in a way that emphasizes these awakenings that can happen mentally and spiritually, instead of just how many pull-ups you can do.

Dean, leashless, on *Sinister* (5.12), Mill Creek, Utah

Do you consider yourself a spiritual person?

Not in any traditional way of believing in God. I do think there's something else. Maybe it's collective consciousness or something. I don't really have defined views on that. I don't even know what *spiritual* means. But I do know that I feel connected to the other people in the world, the earth, the animals. In that way of feeling connected I do feel spiritual. That's what I pursue in all the things I do—to become closer to what is inside of me and how that is inside of everything. In the collective consciousness of the world and all of its life-forms.

How would you hope to be perceived by others?

I think sometimes I'm more standoffish with people who I don't know, and that can be interpreted in a lot of different ways. But I think mostly I want what's great for everybody, and I'd hope to be recognized as a good person, someone who is hoping to do good things in life and to help the people that I'm close to live their dreams.

Do you ever doubt yourself, and how do you deal with that?

I often doubt myself. I think it's a good thing, because if you doubt yourself, then maybe you're not going in the right direction, or maybe you decide you need to try harder. Basically I try not to let doubt hold me back. Because how can I live like that,

allowing myself to be powerless, when to just keep pushing could get me there? And I think that's what climbing has taught me: Even when things seem impossible and you feel like there's no way, if you just keep trying you eventually get there.

How'd you get into BASE jumping and why?

I've always had this dream about flying. When I think of my earliest memory, that's it. Almost daily I'll flash back to that dream. It's kinda weird. I've always wanted to learn to BASE jump, but I'd never actually gone for it. But then my friend, Jose Perrera, died climbing, and it was so sudden, I saw that if I didn't do these things that I wanted to do, I may never get to do them. So pretty much immediately after he died, I started along the path of learning to BASE jump.

And also, I really think that BASE jumping could change climbing. It would be a great way off of big formations and a beautiful way to enchain formations. Because often getting down takes longer than getting up, and it's often the most dangerous part.

Do you think that might be a possibility, BASE jumping being more incorporated into climbing?

Yeah. It seems like it's happening already. In the alpine world it seems the most useful. On *California Roulette* it took me twenty-four hours to get down, but only nine or ten hours to get to the top. It could open all sorts of things in the mountains, as well as other areas of climbing . . . with big wall climbing it would be so much easier to fly off instead of hiking all your stuff down.

What advice would you like to give to younger climbers who may be reading this book?

Anything is possible and all of us, if we open our mind enough, can do anything and not be limited by what's out there. I think climbing is a way to become in tune with these other awarenesses that we have, and that can bring us further than physical things. Also, if you believe in something, you can do it. I really do believe that there's no limit in climbing or what you can do if you focus hard enough.

DEAN POTTER

Jason has climbed some of the highest and most difficult boulder problems ever.

Jason Kehl

If one were to gather a group of climbers, picking out Jason would not be difficult. Jason intends to stand out. At one competition he wore an old-man suit, discarding it to reveal his identity in the final round. He has also been seen shirtless, with his competition number pinned to the skin on his back. Jason often sports a haircut that friends call a "skullet," where the top of his head is shaved, leaving a ponytail in the back. He also enjoys wearing either tiger-striped or white contact lenses, leaving him looking like he's possessed by some other-worldly being. This is the Jason I have known since I was a fifteen-year-old on my first trip to Rifle Mountain Park, when I wondered who owned the big white van with the skull tied to the front bumper. The first time I saw Jason without any of the above, I was astonished by how "normal" he looked. Indeed, when speaking to Jason, he does seem to be just another guy. His climbing pursuits, however, follow suit with his choice of attire, haircuts, and eyewear. Jason has chosen to pursue a very specialized form of bouldering, seeking out those boulders that are very tall, often called "highballs." One could argue that there is a very thin line between highball bouldering and soloing, but regardless, Jason has climbed some of the highest and most difficult boulder problems ever.

Jason started climbing in Maryland, when he was fifteen. Like many climbers of this generation, he started climbing in a gym and eventually graduated to climbing outside. Today Jason has largely eschewed indoor and competition climbing, choosing instead a life on the road in pursuit of tall boulders. Jason is not only a climber but also an artist, and his art is as unusual as the rest of his appearance. He is very interested in the idea of illusion, in climbing and in his art, and he expresses this to me in our interview. He is intrigued by and uses the idea of illusion in every aspect of his life, and this idea is in part what has enabled him to establish first ascents and first boulder ascents of things like *Evilution* (V12), *After Midnight* (V11), *The New Zero* (V13), *The Fly* (5.14d/V14), *The Black Lung* (V13), and *Straight out of Squampton* (5.13+).

Jason on *Evilution* (V12),
Bishop, California

How did you hear about climbing?

My first encounter was when I was quite young. I saw a book in a store about climbing, and I asked my mother to buy it for me. We were on vacation and her response was, "I'm not going to buy you that book. You'll kill yourself." So I wouldn't talk to her for the rest of the trip. I was all pissed. And then she went back and got me the book. I didn't read the book, though, for five years or something. And

then finally I picked it up. It was just a basic climbing book. Other than that, though, I was always going into the woods, climbing up trees, and stuff like that.

What was it about climbing that appealed to you when you saw the book?

Just being in a different place. There are all these sports: baseball, basketball, etcetera. But you're still on the ground. And climb-

JASON KEHL

ing was an escape. You could get up where people don't go and feel things that people haven't felt.

Did you participate in sports before you started climbing?

Yeah. Basic sports that most little kids play. But then in high school I didn't do any team sports. I'm really not a team player. I took karate or something outside of school. I think that helped my climbing because of flexibility. I was always pretty flexible and able to get into weird positions.

Jason Kehl

Height: 5 feet, 8 inches

Weight: 145 pounds

Date of Birth: 10/18/76

Current Hometown: The road

Age of First Climb: 17

Approximate Number of Days Per

Year Spent Climbing: 200+

Hardest Climb: *The Fly,* **Rumney,**

New Hampshire (14d)

Favorite Climbing Area:

Fontainebleau, France

What do you think has attracted you to the taller boulder problems that you've done?

Definitely it's the illusion of danger or fear when I'm in the situation. It's a situation that I've become comfortable with, but it appears to be very dangerous or bold. It's not as bad as it seems to the outside viewer. When you do stuff like that, you pull it off and people think it's crazy, but you in your mind have become accustomed to it. It's just something that people think can't be done or shouldn't be done.

Have you ever gotten hurt?

I actually haven't gotten hurt doing that kind of climbing, but I have been hurt in comps. I blew my ACL last year, and I had surgery to replace my ACL last May with a cadaver ACL. So I'm half a dead man now, in my leg. But that's going good, and that's the only major injury I've had.

So you do these tall boulder problems. Do you solo, or why not?

No. I free soloed when I was young, because there was an area near my house that I used to go to without a partner. They were probably 60- to 70-foot routes. But it's not worth it, I don't think. It's not my mentality. My mentality is more about understanding where I am and the safety of it. And, yeah, maybe there's a chance for injury, but not . . . I think soloing means death if you fail, but with the highball bouldering, it's more like a stunt fall. You can pull out of it. It doesn't necessarily mean death.

Jason escaping the ground, *The Wind Below* (V8), Joe's Valley, Utah

Do you get scared?

Yeah. I get scared all the time. I get more scared on easier highballs than on harder ones.

Why do you think that is?

Because you have more time to think about it. When it's hard, the only thought is the movement and not letting go. But when you're on something easier, you have time to relax, and once you relax, thoughts enter your head. I think that's why a lot of people don't do highballs—because they're sitting there thinking about it. But once you actually get on it and start to learn the moves those thoughts fade away.

Can you tell me a bit about *Evilution*?

It had been climbed to the lip before, by Chris. And I had talked to him and some other people about it, but they just thought it was too tall. They were talking about filling the base with cardboard boxes like you'd see in a stunt movie and bailing into this big mass that would slow you down. I went there and tried the problem to the lip, where you'd usually just drop. And I was just amazed at the wall and wondered why I couldn't try to go to the top. So I tried it for two weeks or so and finally did it.

Has that been repeated?

I think it's been repeated twice maybe, or maybe three times. But it hasn't been repeated the way I went. I went left and up, but there's another way that traverses right and up. We were originally trying it that way,

but it was kinda rotten granite, so I abandoned that way and started going up this other line, which I think is a little harder but is the weakness of the height of the boulder. The boulder swoops down there. It's the groove you would want to go up into.

Why do you think it is that people didn't want to go over the lip?

It was unknown, with potential for a pretty bad fall, and it's high.

So tell me about *The Fly*. Why did you do that without a rope?

I think I wanted to do it without a rope, because the first time that I saw the route I was amazed that this piece of rock was so difficult and so compact—so perfect basically. And I had climbed boulder problems that were a similar height. The landing is a little sketchy, but I thought that it could be done and should be done.

Why do you think it should be done?

Because I don't like clipping bolts. I don't like being distracted by anything. I just want to climb freely. It's about just climbing up something with your own body and not having to think about anything else.

Is there a difference between having a rope and having a bunch of spotters and crash pads?

Yeah, because when you have a rope and the quickdraws and all that, you're con-

JASON KEHL

sciously thinking about it. It's like . . . I was doing some healing for my knee—sensory deprivation—and I kinda relate it to that. Sensory deprivation is where all your senses are blocked off, and that allows you to focus more on what you want to focus on. So if I don't have the rope there to think about, or the harness there for my body to be aware of, then I don't even think about the fall until I'm in the air. All of that is gone from my head, and it's just me and the rock and just trying to get up.

Do you ever climb on a rope?

The last time I climbed on a rope seriously was in the Frankenjura, and I just kinda got tired of it and wanted to boulder for a while.

So what do you do now? Where do you spend most of your time?

On the road. In America, in my van, going overseas. I've been trying to get overseas as much as possible, as well as trying to make it work as a climber.

Do you do anything besides climbing?

Yeah. I do some writing, but mostly shaping holds and doing graphics, ads, catalog designs.

How would you want to be perceived by other people? You have a very unusual style.

I don't want to be perceived. I want to be questioned. I want to keep people guessing.

Why?

You know, you see someone who's in the spotlight or whatever, and you see them all the time. I want people to be constantly questioning what's going on, what I'm doing. I don't want them to be comfortable with the idea of me at all.

Are you afraid of people assuming that they know you?

Maybe. And I think that's kinda why I have this outer persona that isn't really even me. People pigeonhole me into a certain mentality and assume they know me, but in my mind I know that they don't, at all. It's kind of an inside joke. It keeps me sane, I guess.

Where do you see the future of climbing going, or where would you like to see your personal climbing going?

Personally I see myself going climbing with good friends and climbing bigger, badder boulder problems. Push the limit of "normal" bouldering. Recently I went down to Arkansas with a bunch of guys, and we were just looking for the biggest, coolest things we could find. I'd like to have it be more like that—more people traveling and searching for the perfect moment of pushing their own limit. I'm not so much talking about the actual climbing, but the lifestyle of it.

If climbing were to go more in the direction that you are suggesting, then there would be a certain aspect of danger that

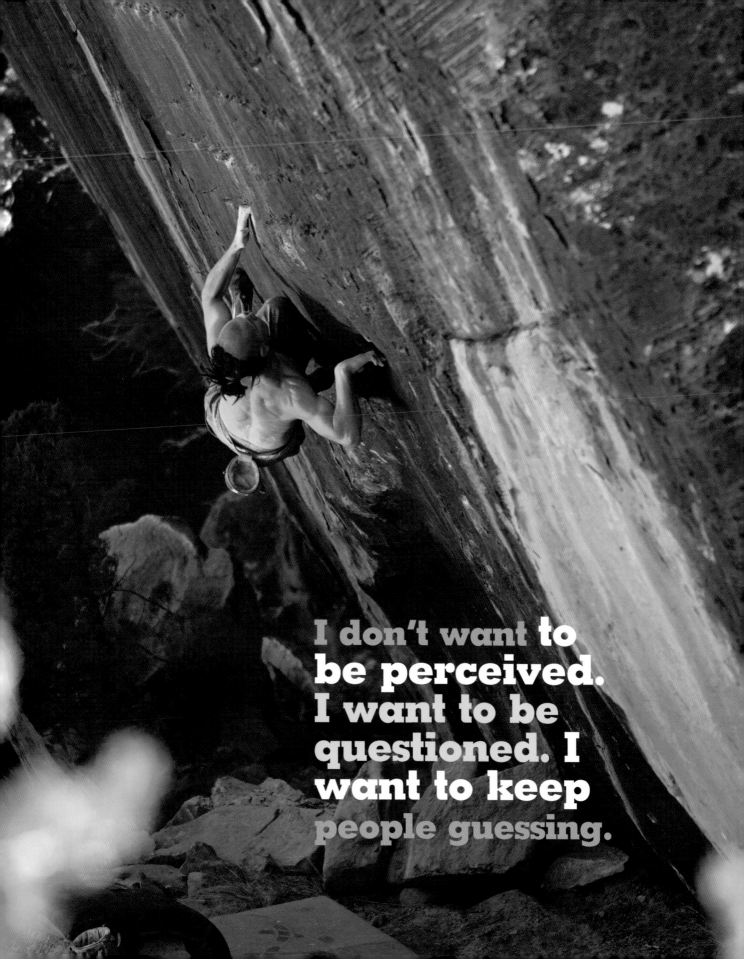

I don't want **to be perceived. I want to be questioned. I** want to keep people guessing.

would limit the number of people willing to participate. Is that something that appeals to you?

To a certain extent. You know, like skate-boarding. You don't want to see people going around in a circle, staying low to the ground. You want to see people exploding off ramps, maybe crashing, maybe breaking their ankle. But they're going for it, and it makes the experience all that more passion-ate, and they're giving their all for the sport.

What goals/plans do you have for the future?

The biggest dream, really, is to keep doing what I'm doing, which is not working too much and climbing as much as I can and being comfortable. Not being a full-on bum, but making it work. And climbingwise, I'm psyched to push myself numberwise, but that's not as important as finding things that leave a lasting impression. I try not to climb just because it's hard or whatever, but because I want to look back at something I did when I'm an old man and be able to say, "Oh wow, I climbed up that. That's crazy."

Do you want to continue your artwork?

Yeah, yeah. For sure.

What's with the dolls?

The dolls. I don't know. That's the real question. What is with the dolls? I think that dolls are one of the weirdest toys that kids can have. Maybe not all dolls, but the

thing is, I go around and I see these bizarre dolls and I'm like, "I cannot believe that someone made this for a child." And that just interests me. It just seems so odd that there are these little rubber humans around. You see some of the ones that I have—and I find them at thrift shops, so you know that someone had to own them—and I'm just like, "If some kid owned this, they're gonna be messed up."

It seems like a lot of your art is death oriented. Why is that?

It's the unknown. Death is unknown. It means something different to everyone, and there's a lot of question behind it because no one knows really where they're going or what's happening. But . . . I don't know why actually.

Do you think that plays at all into the kind of climbing that you do?

Yeah. Probably. I think a lot of people fear death. To think about it, though, helps me become more familiar with it. Another big reason is that if I don't ever think about it, then I'm not going to live my life to the fullest. I consider death an end to what is happening right now, and that pushes me to go out there and do it—now—don't waste time. Everyone's going to die. People who are sitting around watching television need to get out there and do something. Because this is life. This isn't a show where you can just sit there and make yourself comfort-able. You need to go out there and get it. And if you don't, death is going to take you, and you're going to miss your chance.

This isn't **a show where you can** just sit there . . . . You need **to go out there and** get it.

Is there anyone in the climbing community who has been an inspiration or role model for you?

When I started climbing, the guy that I was amazed by was a Spanish climber named Jordi Salas. I climbed with him a lot and learned a lot from him. He was a great climber—still is. He always had a good attitude. He's kinda into soloing a little now, too, so I think we have a similar mentality.

What do you think drives people to solo?

I just think it's a different world. It's an escape, and if you have the mentality to do that then you are going to be in a place that a lot of people will never experience. It might be an addictive feeling, like a drug.

You said that the idea of having an escape is what attracted you to climbing. Why do you feel the need to escape?

I feel like humans in general are so foreign to the earth, and I like the idea of getting back to the roots of an animal. If there's a crowd of people, I'm going to be the one who's climbing into the tree. I'm going to be the one who's different, the one who's getting away from all these people in a way that they might not even be able to consider doing. It's a physical skill that I wanted to learn that would allow me to be in a different place, physically and mentally.

Why do you think you need to be different or stand out?

Because I don't like what I see. Most people are in an office or cubicle every day. I don't want to be any part of it, and I'm trying to get as far away as I can.

And you want people to notice that you're doing something different?

Yeah, yeah.

Do you enjoy just climbing?

Yeah, but I don't feel like I just climb. I'm constantly working—on the computer, on my art, on photography. I always—especially in the past couple of years—have jobs that I'm doing. It's cool, because I'm always climbing, but I have other things that distract me.

Have you always been creative? Have you always felt that you were a little different? Like in public school did you dye your hair?

No, no, no. I always thought that I was different, but I tried to do everything not to show it. In high school I wore jeans and a blank T-shirt. No logos, nothing. I wanted to be simple man, simple boy.

Why?

Because, especially in high school, people don't understand that at all. I knew that I wanted to do so much different stuff, but I went to high school up in the farms of Maryland. Agriculture classes, horticulture classes. I was just trying to get through there so I could get out and explode.

Did you always do artwork though?

Yeah, always. Since I was a little kid, I've taken art classes.

What's your favorite kind of art?

Right now I've been doing a lot of photography, digital stuff. Surreal. Stuff that looks real at first, but then you look into it and it trips you up.

Do you think you look at climbing the same way?

Yeah. I like the concept of illusion, and climbing can be an illusion sometimes. Danger can be an illusion. To the climber it isn't there, but to the people watching it is. You can create an illusion so easily. You become a magician.

Did you go to college?

Yeah, I went to community college in Maryland and took every photography class, every drawing class, sculpture class that I could, and then I was done. I wasn't really in it to get a degree, I was more into it to learn some stuff and do my own thing. All the computer skills I've been using to do design stuff were self-taught.

Why climbing?

I like the fact that it's so fine-tuned, and there's so much going on. The ultimate experience in climbing, I think, is when you're in the crux of the hardest thing you've ever tried, and in that one instant nothing else exists except for this that is in front of you. And that is the only thing. The world could be blowing up, and it doesn't matter. It's pure focus.

Climbing outside vs. inside?

To me, gym climbing is climbing, but it's not real climbing. It comes and it goes. You don't have any solid achievements to look back on that are real. You do a route outside and it's gonna be there forever, and people are going to come try it.

So it's another form of creativity.

Yeah, totally. It's a form of creativity; it's a form of leaving your mark. I want to go out and do cool lines so that anyone who comes to the area will see that particular problem and it will stand out among all the others. That's the one they want to try. That's the problem they can't believe has been done. That will be there forever. When we're dead.

How do you feel the second you top out?

It's like climax, you know. It's the best feeling. It's what you've been working for. You imagine that feeling when you're trying the first moves.

Is that what you're working for? That feeling?

Yeah, that feeling. The goal.

JASON KEHL

When you're actually climbing, in there, doing it, are you still thinking about the finish?

No, not so much. There's so much going on that you can't. You need to focus on that 1 square foot in front of you. If you think about the top, maybe you'll fall.

How does it feel after the fact?

Sometimes you wish it wasn't over, because the feeling when you're on the ground and you've worked all the moves and you know you're going to send, that's a good feeling too. It's not just about succeeding, it's about the process.

Does it make you nervous?

Yeah. But the more you think about it—it's like jumping off the high diving board or something—the more you sit there and think about it, the worse off you're going to be.

For the kind of climbing that you do, what do you think is the most important skill to have?

Concentration. Fitness, obviously, but you need to be right there. You can't be on the route or problem and thinking about the landing, or anything else. You just have to be where you are. Having past successes also helps. Confidence. Confidence is a great thing. And you know when you don't have it.

Have you ever had an instance when you've managed to do something without that confidence?

Yeah. That's why I think it's better to not have an idea of the outcome. Just going and seeing what happens. That's the only way you can surprise yourself. Not fearing failure or success.

More Climbers to Watch

Paul Robinson

Date of Birth: 8/28/87

Years Climbing: 8

Hometown: Moorestown, New Jersey

Known For: Bouldering

On *The Fly* did you work it on a rope before doing it?

Yeah, but I never sent it on a rope. I wasn't planning on sending it on the rope. I was just working the crux and stuff. The day that I stuck the crux, I stopped climbing and pulled the rope. That kinda blurs the line between the different forms of climbing, because people don't know if it's soloing or what it is. But if you think about it, it's really all the same. Some boulder problems you can get a friend to push you up and try a move, or sometimes there's a slab behind you so you can pull on higher up. Or maybe you can rappel down something and feel the holds. I don't see anything wrong with any of it. There aren't any rules.

On *Evilution* did you try the top somehow before doing the problem?

No, but I did rap down and clean it.

Do you like repeating stuff, or would you rather put up something new?

Well, I like repeating stuff, but it's fun to go out with friends and brush something up. It's more fulfilling, I think, to put up something new. There are no expectations, no ratings, you're just into it for the beauty of the line or the feature you see, and you just want to figure it out. It's a purer thought process, I think, in your head. It's simpler, and it's awesome.

What would you want to pass on to younger climbers?

To constantly move forward and not quit—a lot of people will decide something isn't for them or that they can't do it, but the people who excel in the sport aren't necessarily the best, they're the people who just don't quit.

Do you think it's a sort of dishonesty to project an image to younger climbers who might be looking up to you that isn't really you?

No, because a video or something they see isn't reality anyway, no matter what image I project.

JASON KEHL

He . . . seems to feel a bit abashed that he has **been chosen** to be part of this **book. His** accomplishments however, speak **for themselves.**

Josh Wharton is a self-professed trustafarian. "Well, a mild one," he says. This small stroke of luck has certainly helped him pursue his passion of alpine climbing at a young age. But money alone will not peaks bag.

Josh was born in Nottingham, New Hampshire, in 1979. His father was a climber, and an accomplished one, before him. But as a child, Josh was not interested in climbing. He tells me, smiling, that he was a "kinda chubby kid," so climbing did not come naturally to him. His first climbing experience was in Wales, the birthplace of his father. A nine-year-old Josh was taken up several slab climbs as an introduction to the sport, and he relates that he would cry at the base for an hour before finally being convinced to go up.

Josh is tall. When I'm introduced to him, he towers over me. He wears a black T-shirt and Mammut climbing pants and looks solid—he's definitely no waif sport climber. Josh and his longtime girlfriend, Erinn, recently moved to Rifle, Colorado, where they own a small house "complete with picket fence," he tells me when I phone to get directions. He has a self-deprecating sense of humor and seems to feel a bit abashed that he has been chosen to be a part of this book at all. His accomplishments, however, speak for themselves.

Josh started climbing seriously while in high school. He started going with some friends, and finally took a liking to the sport. After high school he moved to Boulder, Colorado, to attend college, and at the same time discovered that he had landed in a climbing mecca. He spent the next several years devoting his time to climbing, with a little school in between. Since then Josh has established himself as one of the premier alpine climbers in the world. His list of accomplishments is too long to list, but two of them stand out among the others.

In the summer of 2002, Josh and partner Brian McMahon made a bold ascent of *The Flame* in northeastern Pakistan. The team went in spite of strong warnings against doing so, due to political instability. Their trip came on the heels of the bombing of the World Trade Center, and fear of terrorism was at an all-time high. Josh and Brian were the only climbers in the valley during their two-and-a-half-month trip, and they had their sights set on the only unclimbed peak in the area, which had been tried, unsuccessfully, on multiple occasions by many established alpine climbers. Undeterred by this, or by the possibility of political instability, they fought through bad weather and numerous setbacks before finally succeeding. One of the more impressive feats of the ascent was Josh's lead on the final pitch of the route, a 165-foot slab that offered no protection. *American Alpine Journal* editor John Harlin wrote about this accomplishment, saying that it was "one of the boldest summit bids in climbing history."

Josh did not stop there, however. In 2004 he and climbing partner Kelly Cordes upped the ante by climbing a route that is considered to be the longest route in the world. The southwest ridge of the Great Trango Tower stood 7,400 feet and had never been climbed. Josh and Kelly decided to climb it alpine-style and suffered through not only dropping half of their rack, but also running out of water on the second day of their climb. They were forced to spend the final two and a half days without food or water on a route that left them no option for retreat.

Clearly Josh has amazing skill, fortitude, and bravery in the mountains. To him, however, none of the things he's accomplished would have been possible without the partnerships with other climbers that he's forged along the way.

Josh Wharton

Height: 5 feet, 11 inches

Weight: 170 pounds

Date of Birth: 2/2/79

Current Hometown: Rifle, Colorado

Age of First Climb: 10

Approximate Number of Days Per Year Spent Climbing: 250

Hardest Climb: *Azeem Ridge*

Favorite Climbing Area:

Black Canyon

The Interview . . .

So how did you get into alpine climbing?

I don't know. It just seemed like a natural progression for me. All the biggest, best routes that I wanted to do were in the mountains.

Was your dad more of an alpine climber? For most people of our age group, the natural progression might be more along the lines of doing harder sport routes or something.

Well, I was thinking about that yesterday. There really aren't that many people my age alpine climbing. I think the reason is that these days kids start climbing in the gyms, or sport climbing, or bouldering. And when you're really good right off the bat, you get sucked into chasing numbers. You just don't get interested in doing big

97

stuff in the mountains—partly because to climb big alpine routes you need to get experience. You need to put in a lot of time climbing long 5.9s in the mountains, for example. You can't try things that are hard right off the bat.

What is it about alpine climbing that you were attracted to?

The partnerships that come out of it. You really develop a solid connection with your partner. And I really enjoy the commitment aspect of it. I feel like I climb better in the mountains, because there's that sense that you really only have that one chance to do it. With a sport climb you can always come back and try it again, but with alpine climbing, you might go for a month and only have five days of good weather. So on those five days, you really need to climb your best and do the best that you can in the situation that you're given.

How do you support your climbing habit?

Well right now I've got a gig with Mammut, and they're giving me some money—helping me with trips and stuff. And I'm a mild trustafarian, so that helps a lot. I mean, I'm definitely not the kind of trustafarian that gets to spend at will, but on a climber's budget, I can survive. I was also doing a lot of freelance writing for a while, but I haven't come up with anything interesting in a while.

Did you go to school?

Yeah, I went to CU and majored in English literature, which basically means I majored in climbing. The last couple years of school, I set up my classes on a Tuesday/Thursday schedule so that I could go climbing all the time.

You are one of the less-known climbers in the book. Have you intentionally stayed out of the limelight?

I used to think the whole sponsorship thing was ridiculous, but then I realized that if I wanted to continue climbing and going on trips, I would need to find a way to make that possible. So lately, within the last two years or so, I've been pursuing it a bit. And I've been pretty lucky. There are so many really good climbers out there that I feel really fortunate that it's working out for me. I've got a really good deal going on with Mammut right now. And you know, there's all this talk about "soul" climbing, especially in the alpine circle, and I actually think a lot of that is people being like me— not wanting to put the work in that it takes to get it done, or to reciprocate to the person giving them stuff.

I think it was interesting back when big wall climbing was really big. There were all these highly publicized ascents on alpine walls. People were taking laptops so they could write into their Web sites while they were doing it. There was a lot of ridiculous stuff like that. And I thought that was lame, because it was basically guaranteeing the outcome of the climb. But obviously the media liked that, because they were pretty likely to have success. If you put a bunch of money into a climb, then it's

Josh routefinding on the
Azeem Ridge, Great Trango
Tower, Pakistan

I feel like I climb better in the mountains . . . because there's that sense that you really only have that one chance to do it.

pretty likely that whomever you're sponsoring is going to make it. But doing things alpine-style, it's impossible to have any guarantee that you're going to make it, no matter how much money you put into it. So I feel really lucky that people have been willing to support trips that I've been on. You know, because I might go on a six-week trip and the weather's bad the whole time or the route seems too scary, and we don't climb anything. And to find someone who's willing to help us go do that is really pretty amazing.

Do you see yourself climbing more as a career in the future?

Well I think climbing as a career is a joke, really. There's not enough money in it. I mean, there's this huge bundle of people in the States who are really good climbers, but then there's a tiny handful of people who are really, really talented. And that handful of people might be able to make it work. Someone might be able to throw them an actual income that they can live on, but I don't really see that happening for me. Regardless, though, I'll continue climbing and going on trips and trying to make it happen as long as it's fun.

What is your feeling on the style in which you do a route?

Style is important to me. I'm maybe not as die-hard about it as other people. I know it's really important to Kelly. He would never go on a trip with a person he considers to have bad style.

I think what's most important to me stylewise is cleaning up after yourself. The

problem with big expedition-style projects is that people tend to leave fixed ropes, tents, and all kinds of things. And that's a bummer. You know, you go to this amazing place in the middle of nowhere, and there's trash all over a ledge or fixed lines hanging on a route that you want to climb. For example, there's this wall in India, a big, big 700-meter north-facing wall. And there had been a whole series of alpine-style attempts in the past, and siege-style, and the Russians took a team of twenty and fixed the whole thing. But they ended up leaving a lot of fixed gear on the route. To me, I think it's an amazing accomplishment that they pulled it off and made it to the top, but at the same time it sucks that they left all those fixed ropes there. If someone wants to go make an alpine-style attempt, it's not going to be the same if you're climbing next to a fixed rope and you have that way to bail off. It kinda detracts from the experience.

The Southwest Ridge of the Great Trango Tower—what made you want to climb it?

I had been to Pakistan twice before and was interested in it, but I always had other objectives. I came home from that second trip, though, knowing that the next time I went that's what I wanted to try.

Did you know Kelly very well before you guys went?

No, not super well. I gave a slideshow for the American Alpine Club about *The Flame,* and after the show Kelly came up to me

asking a lot of questions, so I knew he was interested in going. We had probably only climbed half a dozen times together before we went, but I knew he was a great guy and I really liked him. And for me, going on an alpine trip, it doesn't really matter how hard you climb. It's more important by far that you get along with your partner, because you're going to be spending a lot of time together. So I like going on trips with people who are interesting and fun. And Kelly is really fun to hang out with but also a really good climber.

Why did you decide to do the route alpine-style?

I guess because the thing is so huge . . . well, for one I'm kinda lazy. I don't really like the whole big wall thing—fixing ropes, hauling bags, all that. So that's kinda fast-tracked me toward alpine-style climbing. And alpine-style is more fun, I think, than big wall-style. I mean, a lot of people talk about how it's much more of a purist, hard-core experience than big wall, but in reality, it's just way more fun to have noth-

JOSH WHARTON

Taking a day off from climbing, Rocky Mountain National Park

ing but a little backpack while you're climbing. It's more like going to the crag. So I guess it's the only way I ever considered doing that route. I never really consider trying anything big wall-style, but that route in particular would be a lot more work. For example, the wall is really low angle at the bottom, so the hauling would be atrocious. And it would just be an endless process. I mean, the two routes to the left of ours were month-long projects.

Early on in the route, you guys dropped a bunch of your cams. What went through your mind when that happened?

Well I think we lost seven cams out of twenty, and I just thought, "Well, it'll be a little harder now." We were just so excited about the climbing that we weren't thinking about going down at any point. We just knew that we were going to have to make do and make it work somehow. Dropping the cams was definitely serious, but we still knew we could make it happen.

On routes like that, what finally makes you decide that you have to go down? I mean, understandably, you really want to do the route and you go through some amazing things to get there, but what is the breaking point?

I don't know. I've been really lucky on trips that I've been on, to have good weather and good partners and good situations. I haven't had too many times where I've had to bail or where it was a tough call. I just did a trip this last winter to Patagonia, and at one point we had to climb in a waterfall because a snow mushroom was melting. We all got really cold, particularly me, because the belay was in the waterfall, and I was completely hypothermic. At that point we had to make the decision to go down, because we'd freeze if we had to stay overnight. But we wound up drying out, so we decided to bivy and continue up the next day. So it just always depends—I guess the decision is based on weather, how committed you are, and how difficult it would be to bail as opposed to continuing on.

On the Southwest ridge, for example, we got to a certain point where the route is actually horizontal. There are quite a few gendarmes for 1,500 feet or so, so at a certain point it would have been just as hard, if not impossible, to retrace your steps as it would have to summit and go down the descent. So you're basically fully committed. You have to go over the top.

And how's that feeling, knowing that you can't turn around?

I feel like I climb really well when I feel that way. Because no matter what presents itself, your only choice is to climb up it because there's no other option. I think that was actually one of the really cool things about that route. It's the only route I've done like that—where you're fully committed and there's no bailing.

I read that you ran out of water. Tell me about that.

One of the nastiest things about that route was that we ran out of fuel about halfway up, so we had no water for the last fifty hours. We were just totally parched for the last two days.

What is that like, being that drained?

You're just completely worked. Jugging a pitch, for example, you do five strokes and then have to rest your head on the rope for five minutes. And then you repeat that. We were totally trashed.

How do you deal with the elements of danger or fear that alpine climbing has?

I guess I am drawn to routes that make me nervous about doing them. I like going and doing something that I don't think I can necessarily succeed on.

Why is that?

Because there's a unique challenge to that kind of climbing. There are a lot of different components that have to go into it. The satisfaction you get out of accomplishing something like that is amazing, and to me it lasts a lot longer than say, doing a route at your local crag. Like the route on the Great Trango—the fact that I realized that once we got up there we were going to be fully committed. But I'm kinda drawn to the challenge of doing routes like that.

But also, you put so much into a route like that. It's not just packing your bag and trying the route. It's organizing the trip, buying the tickets, figuring out your porters, traveling a week or ten days just to get to your base camp. Everything that goes into it really makes it so much more rewarding. You meet so many interesting people along the way, and it's such a beautiful place. It's just that much more rewarding. So when you get into a scary situation, you're more willing to go for it, because you've put so much into it. I'm more willing to go for it on a route in Pakistan, even though the consequences are bigger, than I am maybe cragging at the pass or trying to run it out at Rifle.

When you're on a route like that, is the summit always in your head?

It's one pitch at a time. You're always rationalizing your situation as you go. What is this next bit looking like? What are we going to do if weather moves in? You're always thinking ahead or thinking what the next piece of the puzzle is, rather than just trying to get to the summit.

How much do you usually know about a route before you start it?

It depends. On the Great Trango, for example, we knew a fair bit because Timmy O'Neill had tried it before, and you can look at it really well. So we kinda knew what to expect—what was at the steep part, what the lower-angle stuff would be like, etcetera. But then this route, *The Flame,* that I had done a couple of summers before, we knew nothing about. That route was cool because it has a wall that looks like Half Dome, and there's a little spire on the top of it. And from binoculars at the base, it didn't look like there were any cracks on the spire, so we didn't know for sure if we were going to be able to climb that spire at all.

That trip was actually, in some ways, the coolest trip that I've ever been on. It was doing *The Flame* that made me think "This is what I want to do."

Why was that?

Well I went with my friend, Brian, the summer after 9/11. Nobody was in Pakistan. We saw two other white people for ten weeks, and it was a really incredible experience. We applied for the Muggs Stump grant, and they really liked our proposal but didn't think there was any way we were going to go to that part of the world. Everybody was freaking out about terrorism, and there was a lot of nuclear tension between India and Pakistan. There had been a terrorist attack on the Indian Parliament, and they were saying that it had been Pakistani-Kashmir liberal freedom fighters. So it was just a totally wild

Josh reveling in the last moments of
daylight, Patagonia, Argentina

experience to go over there and try and do
that climb.

    We were the only people at Shipton
Base Camp for two months, and it rained
for the first forty days. So we had ten days
left, and the weather got good. But all this
gear we had cached got crushed by a boulder, so we had to roll the boulder and dig
it out. There was just this series of incredibly unfortunate events, and yet we still
wound up doing the route and it was really
rewarding and really cool. In fact the crux
of the route was the last pitch, which was a
160-foot 5.10 slab, and we had no bolt kit,
so it was 160 feet of 5.10 with no gear.

Do you find that you thrive on setbacks?

Yeah, kind of, because it's so rewarding, so
amazing. Maybe, on these routes that I've
done, if we hadn't actually done them,
then I would have said that I'd never do it
again. If I'd sat there for forty days in the
rain and hadn't gotten to climb, but I
learned so much on the trip to do *The
Flame,* because it was so interesting to see
the way that central Asia was represented
in the media versus what it was like when
you were out there. You know, the truth is
that 99 percent of the people you meet are

JOSH WHARTON

Josh during his and Jonny Copp's winter speed ascent of *The Diamond*, Logs Peak, Colorado

really nice, kind, and caring. People don't see that because all you see on the news is the negative, so people wind up thinking it's terrible. (Although I'm sure Beth and Tommy might say differently, since they had a bad experience.)

How is it often being the youngest climber on a trip?

I've been the youngest, but not by a lot. It's not really anything. It doesn't really affect anything either way, although maybe my partners have been more impressed by what I've done just because I'm that much younger. Maybe they've been a little more surprised by it on our trips than they would have been if I had been their age.

Why do you think there aren't more young people alpine climbing?

I'm not sure, although it's really interesting. If you think about amazingly talented rock climbers like Chris Sharma or Dave Graham—if those guys got into alpine climbing, they could do amazing stuff. But there's a mental element to alpine climbing that maybe some people have and some people don't as much. Sometimes by being a less-talented rock climber I had an advantage for going alpine climbing. I wasn't thinking, "Oh God, I'm going to be sitting in a tent for two months. I'm going to be so out of shape. I'll be terrible when I get back to Rifle. I won't be able to redpoint anything." And there are a lot of people who aren't willing to go and not climb for two months. It's a tough thing. It's also

hard to be away from Erinn for two months and not be able to see her or talk to her. Those things are cruxy, and I think that's why a lot of people aren't as interested. They often say alpine climbers do their best stuff when they're getting divorced or things are going terrible in their life—because it's easy to run away from their life and be fully committed to what they're doing. I'm hoping I don't wind up like that.

How would you hope to be perceived by others?

I guess I'd just like to be seen as a nice guy, more than anything else. I always think it's really interesting how once you get involved in the whole clique of climbing, you know everybody and it's such a small world in some ways. And once you get linked in the media part of it, it feels like that's a self-perpetuating cycle. You know, for example, being friends with the folks in the mags makes all the difference whether or not you get in there. Like when I did *The Flame,* it got hardly any press compared to the *Azeem Ridge.* And I think that's because I had alpine climbing for that much longer, so more people knew me, and also Kelly has been climbing for a long time and knew a lot of people. So instantly *Alpinist* wants an article from us when we get back and knows about our route. So I guess where I'm going with this is that people read about you in the mags and they assume, "Oh, you're in the mags, you must be super rad." And that's definitely not the case. There are so many good climbers out there, and a lot of them you never hear about at all. And I think it's pretty typical

JOSH WHARTON

If you really want to do something and you really work hard for it, you can.

in our society, this whole hero-worship thing that goes on. People assume that they can't do something because other people who get a lot of press have done it. And I don't think that's the case. I think people can do what they put their minds to. If you really want to do something and you really work hard for it, you can. At least within climbing.

What accomplishment are you the most proud of?

Probably *The Flame*. Within climbing, anyway.

What made it different from the other route?

I guess what made it different was—well, the political element was a big part of it. And all the little things—the little barriers— that we had to get past in order to make that climb happen. Even just the act of going. Because literally, CNN was flashing "India and Pakistan on the brink of nuclear war" the day before we left. I mean, Brian didn't even tell his mother that we were going until ten days before we left. So it just felt serious from the get-go. That peak is just so beautiful, and we were really just a couple of gumbies at that point. I had a

picture of that route on my walls for years before doing it.

What are your goals?

My future goals for climbing are to have fun and go on trips that challenge and inspire me. I've got a couple of specific objectives in mind, but it's bad luck to pre-spray too much.

Is there anyone that you've looked up to or been inspired by?

There are a lot of great folks that I've been really fortunate to learn from and be inspired by. Nobody operates in a vacuum, and I've been lucky enough to share a rope with some truly great climbers. The list is huge, but a few of the more important people are Jonny Copp, Mike Pennings, Brian McMahon, Kelly Cordes, Phil Gruber, Chip Chace, and Chris Goplerud. There are also people that I've never climbed with but who continually open my eyes to what is possible in the mountains: Nathan Martin, Bruce Miller, Steve House, and the late Alex Lowe. My dad has also been a huge source of support and wisdom—and probably the biggest influence on my climbing.

JOSH WHARTON

I'm always inspired to work really hard and get better at those things that I'm not naturally good at.

If asked, Steph Davis would swear that she has no natural abilities, whatsoever, for rock climbing. In spite of her eternally pessimistic view regarding her climbing skills, however, she has managed to rise to the top of her sport. Not only that, but she has set records and broken barriers in more than one genre of climbing.

Steph was born in Illinois but spent her childhood and youth moving between several northeastern states. She could not have grown up in a world further from that of rock climbing or sports. Her childhood days were spent either behind a piano or with her nose in a book. Raised in a very academic environment, athletics were not a priority, or even an afterthought, for Steph.

In 1996 she was a freshman at the University of Maryland, and it was there that she got her introduction to climbing. She began mountain biking and in it, her first athletic pursuit, found that she was discovering a new world of friends, experiences, and lifestyles that appealed to her. Soon she was asked by a friend if she wanted to go rock climbing. Steph had never heard of the sport, but she was more than willing to try it. Since that day, she has believed that there is something in people that, if they're lucky, lets them find the thing that they love. Steph was one of the lucky ones, and she found her "thing," on Groundhog Day, in Maryland, at the age of eighteen.

Today Steph is the second woman to free-climb El Cap in a day, the first woman to free-climb *The Freerider* on El Cap, a member of the first one-day ascent of Torre Egger in Patagonia, and the first woman to summit Torre Egger. Ask her how she has managed these things, and she'll tell you: in a word (or two), hard work.

The Interview . . .

Did you like climbing right away?

I did. I was really bad at it, in my opinion. I was doing 5.2, and it was too hard. We're talking 20-foot topropes, and I was really bad at it.

And you liked that? That you were really bad at it?

I did. I've always been like that. There are a lot of things that come really easy for me, but I don't respect them in some ways. For example, I read really fast, I'm good with languages, I was really good in school, good at standardized testing, stuff like that, but I didn't respect it because it came easy for me. I'm always inspired to work really hard and get better at those things that I'm not naturally good at. That is usually what drives me—if something isn't easy, if I flail a little bit.

What else initially attracted you?

I think just that it was totally different. I had spent my whole childhood as a musician. I started playing piano when I was three and the flute when I was nine. I was also really academic, a big reader and studier. So for me, climbing represented a completely different world, and I could see right away there were completely different people doing it. It just seemed really attractive.

So you got through college, and then what?

I finished my undergrad and got a master's in literature. After that I was pretty much expected by my parents to either get a PhD or a law degree. Anyway, I had graduated and was living in Estes Park—that's actually where I met Dean—and I was waiting tables for the summer. I didn't really know what to do next. I had applied for PhD programs and had gotten accepted to some. But I don't know, I just didn't want to go and it didn't feel right. I just wanted to wait tables and climb. And this was a huge rebellion in my family. Huge. There was no understanding or support from my parents. They kept giving me all these dire warnings about what was going to happen to me, so I got really scared. I had previously taken the LSATs and been offered scholarships to several law schools. One of the law schools that accepted me was Boulder. So there I was in Estes, waiting tables, having a tumultuous relationship with Dean, and I got really scared about ruining my whole life. I started thinking that since I did really well on the LSATs, maybe that meant I should be a lawyer. Maybe I had an apti-

tude and would really enjoy it. I thought I had better try, because if I didn't then I would never know. So at the last possible moment, I accepted. I went for a week, and I could just immediately see that I didn't want to do it. Immediately. So I just quit and went to Rifle. And then I knew which path I wanted to take.

To just wait tables and rock climb?

Yup. And it was great, because had I not done that, I think I would always look back and wonder if I should have done those three years of law school. For example, the path that I've chosen is an uncertain lifestyle, but going to law school would have potentially been a very fulfilling career. But I don't think those things. Because I went and tried it, and it wasn't what I wanted.

So was that a defining experience for you?

Yeah, it was huge. Pretty traumatic. My parents freaked out, and I broke up with Dean. Huge chaos.

How old were you?

I think I was twenty-three. That was such a hard time. Early twenties can definitely be tumultuous.

When did you end up doing your first trip to Patagonia?

I went to Patagonia for the first time in the winter of 1996. I had decided to base out of Moab pretty quickly after the whole law school debacle, so I was there the next season to wait tables.

I was friends with a guy named Charlie Fowler. He just happened to love all the same kinds of climbing that I did, so we became friends and started climbing a lot together. He thought I would love Patagonia. And you know how when you see pictures of Patagonia it's all pretty and clear and blue? Of course I thought it looked great. So he convinced me to go. I mean, if people actually know what it's like then they usually don't want to go. But I thought it sounded great. So that winter, when everyone in the restaurant business in Moab gets laid off for the season, I went.

Steph Davis

Height: 5 feet, 5 inches

Weight: 120 pounds

Date of Birth: 11/4/72

Current Hometown: Moab, Utah

Age of First Climb: 18

Approximate Number of Days Per Year Spent Climbing: 200

Hardest Climb: Free-climbing the Salathe

Favorite Climbing Area: Indian Creek

So was that your first alpine experience?

Well I had been pretty excited about the Diamond when I lived in Estes, which is kinda like sport-alpine. I just adored it, and so did Dean. That's actually where we met—on the Diamond. It wasn't alpine climbing, but it gave me a taste of what alpine climbing might be like. I don't think I had done anything else that could remotely be called alpine climbing though. I barely knew how to put on crampons.

And how was it, putting on crampons?

It was . . . I had a really hard first trip. I was down there for about three months, and the entire time was absolutely shit weather. I just went crazy. Always in the past with climbing, if I wanted to climb something I would just go until I could—I would just make it happen. But in Patagonia you can't. Plus I'm the kind of person who always has to be doing something, like running or climbing or gardening. Something. But down there you're in a tent and you can't do anything. And when I was younger I was even worse, so I was just a mess.

We tried really hard to do something in spite of weather, though, and just got super-spanked. We just got the full Patagonia schooling. I came home and got mono, because I was so exhausted. Anyway I had a really intense first trip.

What kept drawing you back?

When I first went to Patagonia, I had just begun to devote my life to climbing. It was

. . . I'm the kind of person who always has to be doing something, like running or climbing or gardening. **Something.**

Steph making *Death of a Cowboy* look easy, Indian Creek, Utah

mostly specifically rock climbing, but I had been very intent on learning the skills involved and had worked really hard and felt like I had gotten pretty good at what I was doing. I thought that I knew what was going on. But in Patagonia that first time, I realized the depth and breadth of knowledge and skills that I hadn't even touched, and I knew I had SO much more to learn. It was a huge eye-opener.

Also, Patagonia is just the most intense place I've ever been. It's terrifying and huge and exhausting. You're always organizing or planning or trying or doing. It's all encompassing. You come home afterward, and real life seems so easy and nice.

How come you've never written about your ascent of Fitzroy?

You know how you get good at a place after a while? I was pretty good at Patagonia, because I had been going down there for five years, and I was obsessed with climbing Fitzroy. And so this poor guy who said he would climb with me, he had never climbed in Patagonia, and he had never really climbed in bad situations. He had done a lot of stuff in the Alps, but in the Alps you wait until it's good and then you go climb, and if it's bad, you leave. It's totally different than Patagonia, where it's epic. So we got on Fitzroy together and even before the weather got bad, the route was out of condition—wet and a mess. He thought we should go down, but I just blatantly said, "No. We will not go down. Just give me the gear and we are going up." He was a great climber and a great guy, but he was just out of his element. And he didn't expect that I would say, "No. We're not

going down, ever." So I think—I mean, if we would have died or something, or if he had, well, that's not really right to force someone, especially when you don't really know them. It's different if you know the person and have a partnership and that whole dynamic. For example, if one person feels weak but the other person wants to go on and consequently carries the team.

But we were strangers. It worked out OK, because he had never been forced to push himself that far, and later, just before the summit, he said, "I'm so happy. I feel better. I'm so glad we didn't go down." But I feel bad about it in some ways. I made him do something that he didn't want to do. I felt bad about that for a long time. And don't get me wrong, I thought he was rad. He pushed himself harder than he ever thought he could, and he did it, and we did it together, and he kicked ass. But to write a story about the moments of the climb? . . . it was one of my most meaningful experiences, but sometimes you don't need to write about those.

So when you started to devote yourself to climbing, did you see yourself going anywhere with it?

I've never considered myself a very good climber, ever. I wasn't great, or even good, right off the bat. I always felt that I had to try really hard and work really hard to make progress. So I would see climbing magazines and think that I would never be able to do that. It seemed ridiculous to ever be a professional climber. And honestly, I've always felt conflicted about making my living from climbing. To me it was this saving path and how I wanted to find my spirituality, so I always had negative feelings when I thought about the concept of people making a living from climbing. And I still struggle with that.

What accomplishment are you the most proud of?

It's funny, because people have been asking me that a lot recently, I think because of *The Freerider*, people expect that that will be my answer. But I don't know. You know how different things happen to you at different times and have a big impact on you? Well obviously doing El Cap was really special and a big accomplishment for me. It was something that I had to work really hard for and meant a lot to me. But in some ways . . . when I was still really young, twenty-four I think, I went to Kyrgyzstan and ended up, really spontaneously, doing a solo route on that trip. I didn't really know how to do it, didn't plan on it. It was just something that I wondered if I could do. I just went and tried, and I was scared. It was a huge accomplishment for me and a very strong experience. While it wasn't technically the hardest thing I've ever done, it's probably the thing I'm most proud of.

How did you feel about approaching such a huge project as *The Freerider* by yourself?

Well I do a lot of things by myself. Almost everything. I spend so much time by myself. I've actually been working on that. I've been trying to do more things with other people this year, because I don't think it's

so good to do so much by yourself. So when I started working on *The Freerider* by myself, it was just natural, because I do everything like that.

How did it feel approaching something that big in general? For a lot of people, that would be a huge undertaking.

It was for me, too. I actually didn't see myself ever climbing *The Freerider*. I had been on the route with Dean, and I thought the climb was so hard. Everything about it. The offwidths seemed impossible. The slabs seemed horrific, the crux pitch was reachy, the layback pitch was terrifying. I just thought there was no way. But then there I was in Yosemite, and Dean was doing this, that, and the other, and I was bored. So since *The Freerider* seemed so hard, and it seemed like I sucked really badly at it, of course I thought I should try it some more. And not because I thought I wanted to send *The Freerider,* just because I saw a lot of room for improvement. I don't really have specific goals. I always just want to be a better climber, so I figure if I work on what I'm bad at, then in the end I will be a better climber.

I find that I am much more of a short-term goal person. I just want to do things and not stop until they're done. So to look at something that big . . .

Oh, it's overwhelming. I used to be like that too, actually. I'm a really obsessive person, so if I start doing something, I

Bouldering desert-style,
Crack House, Utah

don't stop until it's done. For school it was staying up all night to finish a paper, or for climbing, trying one climb all day until I sent it. It's been really hard, but interesting for me to learn patience for a big, overwhelming project.

So how did you find the patience for something like *The Freerider*?

I think Patagonia and climbing in the mountains taught me a lot. You have more long-term objectives, and you have to be really accepting, knowing that you're going to work really hard, not because you want to get this or do this or be this, but because you want to work really hard. Often I wanted to climb the climb or get to the top more than I wanted to be doing it. And that's frustrating. But spiritually I don't think things will happen for you if you go about it that way. It was only when I learned how to let go of the outcome and only care about just being there and doing it that things would work for me. I can't be attached to wanting something a certain way or to have done something. Because that's not really what it's about. It's about my style, my effort, my trying. And so that's how I felt on *The Freerider*. I just felt like, "OK, from day one it's very clear that I am not going to free this route. That's understood; I don't have to care about that. I just want to get better on this route."

What motivates you to push yourself to your physical limit?

Part of it is a personality type, I think. I know my brother is the same way. He's an ER doctor and a very driven person—always has to be doing something. And I know I'm

the same way. I actually have to work harder at taking time off. Also, I don't know if it's genetic or taught, but I just like working really hard. So when I want to do something, I am filled with desire. I'm consumed. It's hard for me to stop, and that is actually a weakness, because I'm a really bad overtrainer, overdoer.

Do you find that you like being out of your comfort zone?

Mm-hmm. That is what really interests me. I enjoy doing things that are comfortable or that suit me or that I'm good at, because they're fun, enjoyable, pleasant. And pleasant is great. I like pleasant. But what really interests me is the struggle. And I like to be interested.

You don't find that it frustrates you?

Yeah, I experience frustration.

But you thrive on that?

Kinda. I go through phases where I'll be so frustrated that I'll hate whatever it is that I'm doing and decide to never do it again. But then once I step away, it eats at me, and I always end up wanting to try again.

Were there any moments when you've felt that you couldn't go anymore?

I think that the ability to keep going even when you're exhausted is something I learned in the mountains. For example, when you're in the middle of a big push—twenty-four hours, fifty hours—there are periods when

But what really interests me is the struggle. And I like to be interested.

. . . when I want to do something, I am filled with desire. I'm consumed. It's hard for me to stop. . .

you feel horrible. But it's always in a situation where you have no choice. I mean, what can you do? You can't stop. You can't just quit because you feel too tired. And even if you could, then later when you are recovered, you'll be irate at yourself for quitting. And so you just continue.

At the same time, though, it is different in the mountains, where you just have to endure, where you're going up snow, forever, and each move isn't hard, but you have to keep doing it. To free El Cap meant climbing at my maximum while in my most exhausted state. For me that was a new moment. I knew how to keep going when I only had to go at a certain level. But on El Cap I was trying to figure out how I could go through my exhaustion and then, basically, do the hardest redpoint of my life.

So, I have a good friend who is an ultrarunner, and can I just say that I worship ultrarunners? Anyway, they talk about a point during a run where they "go through a window." It's when they push through their exhaustion and get a second wind. Well when I was up on El Cap trying to figure out how I was going to redpoint this pitch feeling as tired as I did, I thought of her. She had told me that sometimes on runs she has friends who send her their energy to get through really tough moments. And I really believe in that—I feel like I really feel energies and connections, especially with certain people. And I felt her sending me her energy, or at least I thought about her and how she inspires me.

I mean, I don't feel like I'm suited to be a climber. I'm not a naturally talented climber. But I have found that in certain moments, my mind can make my body do things—things that maybe I didn't think it could do. I've climbed with a ton of people and feel like everybody I know is a better climber than me, but I often can do things that other people can't do. So I feel like I have this mental thing or a spiritual thing or some desire or drive—I don't know—but there's something that works, and that's what I felt that time on *The Freerider*. I didn't know how my body could do it, but then this energy that I got enabled me to climb better. And that's neat. And when you experience something like that one time, I think you can always access it again. You realize that it's true and that it works.

What is it that has inspired you in the past to free solo?

Well it's something I can do by myself—since mostly I like to do things by myself. That was the main reason.

Why do you think it is that you do so many things by yourself?

I am just used to spending a lot of time by myself. As a kid I was either reading or practicing piano, and I guess old habits die hard. But also I get really obsessed with whatever I happen to be doing, whether it's gardening, running, climbing, writing, whatever. I think so much and do so much, that it's kind of a distraction sometimes to try and be around others. Being alone seems to be my most comfortable state, and I really don't even notice that I am by myself. I care a lot about my friends, and I actually do like being with people, but it definitely goes against my natural instincts and often drains a lot of my energy. Even

Steph cranking through the crux
of the "boulder" pitch, *Salathe*
headwall, El Capitan, Yosemite
National Park, California

Dean and I take long periods of time apart, sometimes weeks or months, when we are focused on something. I am always thinking about my friends and loved ones, but I just am not always physically with them.

What is your greatest fear within climbing?

Not being able to climb. Because the thing that is extra scary in life is when you are SO happy, you just feel like it could never stay like that. Because nothing ever stays the same. And that's scary.

Would you consider yourself competitive, either with yourself or with others?

That's a hard question. I really dislike competition—a lot. If I'm ever in a situation where I feel competitiveness, I can't deal with it. I just don't do that thing, or I leave . . . I just hate it. I feel like it's really bad and nasty. It often ruins things that could be pure and beautiful.

In our culture there's a constant insistence that you have to be successful. You have to be able to say, "I am this. I did that." It's all so quantified. But not all cultures are like that. I wish that our culture wouldn't teach people that competition is good. And that is actually one reason why I feel really conflicted about the way I make

my living—because it's inherently competitive. That's why I'm getting to be a climber—because I am letting myself be taken in a certain light, which is as though I am better than other people because "I did this." Fostering that image is what enables me to have my lifestyle, and I don't necessarily agree with that.

I think this whole thing about winning and losing is really artificial. To me competition is about winning or losing, succeeding or failing, being better than or worse than—and that is so limited. I think it's much bigger than that. It's about desire and pushing yourself. It's not about being a quantifiable amount better or worse. You can push yourself constantly, and it's not about the result. Competition is about the result, and that's all there is. It's the effort you put into something that matters, not the result. To me that is what is interesting—how much effort I can give or how hard I can try. The result is artificial.

I think that I have always been too fixated on thinking that I don't have any natural gifts for climbing. I have always thought that I wasn't built for it, wasn't genetically predisposed for it, etcetera. But then, as time goes by and I look at the big picture, I've thought, you know what? The biggest gift a person can have if they want to make their dreams come true is the willingness to work really hard. So maybe that's my gift within climbing, or my gift of life.

. . . one of the most influential and groundbreaking boulderers we have **seen yet.**

One day several years ago, I found myself talking to Wills Young on the phone. I will never forget him telling me that his girlfriend had just done her first V8. He said that I needed to come out to Carbondale—where he was living—and try it. That "girlfriend" was Lisa Rands, soon to become one of the most influential and groundbreaking boulderers we have seen yet.

Lisa is petite and blonde, with a determined jaw and welcoming eyes. She is open and honest about who she is and her accomplishments. Lisa has strong shoulders and arms and looks made for power. But what is most noticeable about her are her fingernails, which are nearly always painted bright green or blue.

Lisa is originally from Southern California. She started climbing when she was seventeen "with a boyfriend, of course," she says. When she started climbing, bouldering was still considered practice for "real" climbing. There were no crash pads and very little overhanging climbing. Still bouldering always appealed to her more than any other genre of climbing. She and her boyfriend went bouldering regularly, because it was nearby, but they also spent a fair amount of time in Joshua Tree, Tahquitz, and Suicide. Her early experiences with traditional climbing would also prepare her for future goals.

After graduating college with a geology degree, Lisa moved to Colorado with another boyfriend, Wills Young, and quickly got a job with a geotechnical firm. The job, however, drained her of time and energy, but at the same time her climbing was improving dramatically. Because of the cold winters in

Colorado, Lisa found herself climbing indoors regularly and decided to enter a few competitions. These competitions were to be the turning point for her. She surprised herself—although no one else who had seen her powerful bouldering abilities—by winning several competitions straightaway.

Since then Lisa has been at the forefront of not only American climbing but international climbing as well. By November 2002 she was ranked number one in the world in competitive bouldering after winning two international bouldering contests. By doing this, she became the first American to win an international bouldering contest. At the same time, Lisa was excelling outdoors as well, and she continued to set standards: She was the first American woman to climb V11 and V12 and the first woman to climb two V10s in a day.

As Lisa's skills expanded, so did her horizons, and she discovered herself drawn to a form of climbing that has earned much respect due to the level of danger involved and skill required. Gritstone climbing in England requires not only amazing power and technical skill but also a certain mental strength that is unique to it. Lisa was initially drawn to gritstone climbing as a means of increasing her mental strength, which she feels is one of her weaknesses as a climber. Something about one particular climb, called *The End of the Affair,* intrigued her, but Wills was hesitant. Gritstone climbing involves only the barest minimum of gear and is very serious, especially at the level of difficulty of this particular route. The climb, however, continued to be of interest to her, and she returned two years later to become the first woman to climb E8, the second woman to climb E7, and the first woman to onsight E5/6.

Wills and Lisa now live in Bishop, California, where she is recovering from knee surgery. Lisa looks much younger than her twenty-nine years, but while talking, her wisdom, clarity, and intelligence belie her true age. Her perspective on climbing is not only inspiring, but is one that cannot be found elsewhere.

Lisa Rands

Height: 5 feet, 4.5 inches

Weight: 120 pounds

Date of Birth: 10/21/75

Current Hometown: Bishop, California

Age of First Climb: 17

Approximate Number of Days Per Year Spent Climbing: 50 to 200 depending on injuries and where I'm climbing

Hardest Climb: E8 on gritstone, V12 bouldering

Favorite Climbing Area: Wherever I have just left

The Interview . . .

Have you enjoyed your decision to climb full-time? Is there any part of you that misses the "normal" life that you had before?

No, I don't miss it. Especially now that we have a home base—I feel like I need that stability. For a while we were just shuffling our stuff around storage units and people's houses. When you do that, your mail gets lost all the time and it seems like you're always missing or forgetting something. It's chaos, and I have a hard time focusing on climbing because I end up worrying about all these other things. That was the only time that I missed "normal" life. And you know, I travel so much that I can't really have a pet, so if I want a dog to run with, for example, I have to borrow a friend's. But other than that, I would hate to be sitting at a desk.

LISA RANDS

What was it that you liked about bouldering?

I always joke that it's because I have ADD. Bouldering requires a short focus but really powerful movement. It's interesting, because I started out bouldering, but as a means of route climbing, and then when I had my eyes opened up to bouldering just for bouldering, it was a total transformation. My climbing—for me power comes naturally, but endurance I have to work really hard for, so I've just never really done it. I seem to enjoy trad climbing, but I'm just not particularly good at it. I do like to go out and just do easy multipitch climbing, though. But bouldering—it's so weird. I don't even know how it's happened. I've just been bouldering this whole time. I'm not sure why it works that way—it's just, there's always someplace new to go, or . . . competitions were driving me for a while, but now I feeling burned out on competitions.

How did you get into doing the World Cup?

Well I was doing the U.S. comps, but I kept hearing comments about how American women were pretty strong but nothing compared to European women. And, being me, I was just like, "Hmm, well let's go see if that's true."

What do you mean, "being you"?

I'm very persistent and stubborn. And when I get something in my head, that's it, I'm going to really pursue it. So I kept hearing those comments, and I just had to go

see if it was true. It's not a very fair comment to hear; it's just like somebody saying, "Yeah, what you guys have done is cool, but not really." So I thought, "Alright, let's go represent American women."

And how did it go?

Well, I took second at my first World Cup, and I was pretty happy about that. We'd just had a month of bad weather in Fontainebleau, and that was my training. So the week before the competition, when most people are resting, I just went to the climbing gym a bunch of times to get used to plastic holds. I wan't rested at all for the comp, and I think I got through purely on willpower. It wasn't a pretty sight. I was just doing anything I could to get to the top of the wall. And the European women, they're very stylish.

Were you surprised by how well you did? Was there a part of you that believed what people were saying about the Europeans?

No, because I just know it's not true. I mean, you, Lynn (Hill), Robyn (Erbesfield), and other American women have done really well. I never really thought it was true.

Did you enjoy competing?

I did. At one of the first competitions, oh, it was horrible, it was slabs, and I had just discovered my weakness, and I took eighth. And then the next competition, I don't know, I trained harder and I focused a little better, and I won. That was a big thing for me. But then the next one I entered I won

too. And that one meant a lot as well, because before the finals you were allowed to preview the problems with the other women. So all the women were talking to each other and getting beta, but I don't speak French.

And you were usually the only American?

Yeah, pretty much.

How was that?

Um, sometimes in isolation you feel a little neglected (laughs). Everyone else is there with their trainers, getting a massage or physical therapy. And I'd just be sitting there by myself, wondering, "Excuse me, can I have a little wall space to warm up?" You have to be really assertive, and I usually become the opposite, more timid.

Did you find that the atmosphere was different between comps in Europe and the States?

Mm-hmm. They're very focused in Europe. At first I didn't know anybody and hadn't traveled a lot, so I didn't really understand—every culture is different, and people are a reflection of the country they come from—so I'd walk around at comps, smiling and saying hi to people, and I got some really weird looks. So of course I thought that the other girls didn't like me. But after doing several competitions, I started realizing that they were just shy, and after a while they started opening up and talking to me. Now if I go back to a World Cup, I feel like I know most of the

people and they're all really friendly, but it took a while to understand that.

Why did you say earlier that you're over competing?

Well, I've never considered myself a competition climber. I feel like I'm an outside climber who just started doing some comps. But there was a point when I realized that I'd become a competition climber who was trying to find some time to go outside. I remember being in a climbing gym in England and I heard some guy whisper, "That's Lisa Rands. She's this competition climber." And it just really irritated me, because I'm not a competition climber, I'm an outside climber. I just realized that competitions were taking over my life and dictating my schedule, so I lost some interest.

You were the first American woman to do V11, right? How'd that feel? Did you realize that you'd even done that?

It was a sequence of things. That problem was in Bishop, where we'd moved. There were several problems on that boulder that I really liked, and that one was actually a harder start to a problem called High Plains Drifter. I remember watching Chris Sharma and Wills climbing on it, and in my mind I thought I shouldn't try it. It was too hard. So then Wills convinced me to try it one day, and I eventually realized that it might be possible. For me it was special, because it was finishing off the problems on that boulder that I wanted to climb. And it was

Lisa, fearless on
the gritstone,
United Kingdom

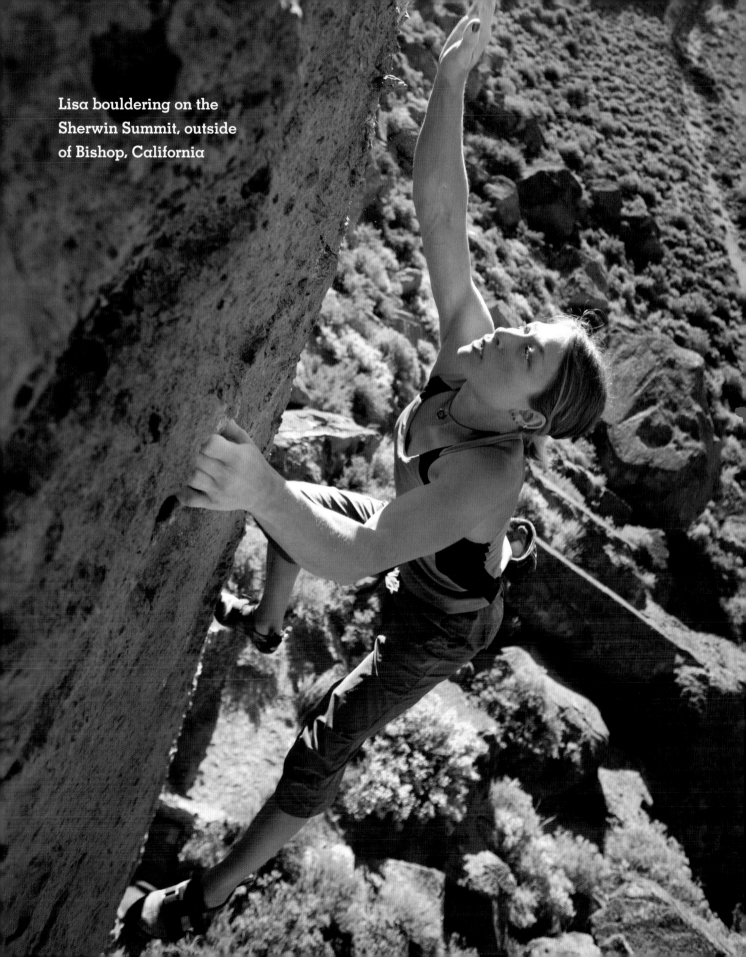

Lisa bouldering on the
Sherwin Summit, outside
of Bishop, California

also just this mental realization that just because I don't think I'm "supposed" to be able to climb something doesn't mean that it's true. I need to get over that, and I think the way I grew up climbing with men, in my mind I always thought that I shouldn't be able to do something if they can't do it. And it's been this real barrier that I've struggled with. That problem was another stepping-stone to overcoming it.

It seems like bouldering involves a lot of failure or falling. Do you find that motivates you or gets you down?

I think that I've kept motivated by trying not to spend a lot of time on one boulder problem. Typically . . . I mean, having said that, I think I did once end up spending five days trying to do something. But I don't like things that I have to get in shape for. I'll lose interest. However, if I try things that I know I can do in a day or two, then I stay motivated. I have friends that get really upset because they're trying something their entire season of bouldering, and if they don't do it, there's this whole feeling of failure. Where they should have gone out and climbed some easier things and gotten their level up a bit higher and then gone back to it.

Within bouldering what do you think is the most important skill to have—do you think it's willpower, fitness, or concentration?

It's a lot of things. And I'm still learning a lot. I used to think it was just trying to get strong, but then I realized I needed tech-

nique, and then I realized that mentally I had to be more focused, and then that I need more flexibility. Now I'm realizing that, just because I might be able to climb one particular style, it doesn't necessarily make me a good climber. I need to then be able to climb on slabs and on slopers. So, for me, I'm trying to become more well-rounded.

I don't believe in just going and trying to tick a hard grade on something that suits me. I don't think that makes you a good climber. It just means that you found something that suits you with a high grade. I want to be able to go to any area, any style of rock, and have that certain base level that I can climb anywhere.

The route in England. How did you end up doing that? Was it your idea, or was it something that Wills suggested?

It definitely wasn't his idea, although he did introduce me to gritstone climbing. The first time I went to England, I just bouldered, and I had a lot of fun because I didn't limit myself to paying attention to grades. We just climbed anything we could—it was summertime and everybody was saying it was so hot, but it really helped my technique. When we went back, I started trying to lead some routes, but I was pretty scared.

My desire to pursue gritstone climbing goes hand in hand with a competition that I did in Boulder. I climbed really strong in the first round, but in the second round I just lost it. Robyn Erbesfield was there, and she told me I needed mental training. Her

LISA RANDS

comment made me realize that I don't need to get stronger in terms of my muscles, I need to get mentally stronger. Gritstone climbing really requires me to control my own mind when I'm climbing, to teach myself to relax if I'm scared. It teaches you how to have that 100 percent concentration when you know you can't fall.

As far as that particular route, I am definitely the one pushing it. Initially when I looked at the route—it's called *The End of the Affair,* the E8—I thought I wanted to go do it and got all excited, but Wills didn't know if he wanted me doing it. He thought I should think it over. So I just left it for two years.

Wow. Two years.

Well the only reason I got on it in the first place was because I had a finger injury and it's open handed. But then I had this weird experience when I decided to solo an E5. The crux is at the bottom, but then you have to keep your head together and continue up a very exposed arête. You can't fall off, because it's an absolutely horrible landing. So I got up onto the arête and basically had one move to do. I was very focused, but then all of a sudden I just lost focus and became aware of my surroundings and where I was. I was leaning in, really close to the arête, and I remember seeing a dead spider in a web. And then I looked around, and I saw all the scenery around me and I just thought, "What am I doing up here?" And I ended up having to down climb. That experience made me realize what a serious position I would be putting myself in if I pursued *The End of the Affair.* The E5 I could down climb, but I

knew that if I tried the other route, I wouldn't be able to down climb, and the crux is at the top. So that's what made me leave it for a while. But when we went back last fall, I was really motivated on it, and I just felt like I was mentally better prepared.

Why do you think you were mentally better prepared?

I think I'd been really trying to work on controlling my nerves—even while bouldering. I quite often climb really rigid and don't relax. I also feel that in the last year I've let go of caring about performing, winning comps, doing hard boulder problems, whatever, and it's just made me feel freer. And suddenly I can focus more on my climbing now.

What do you think brought that on?

I actually think it was having this knee injury. I was always very aggressive before, having to book every minute of my schedule, constantly going, going, going. I'd get an injury, recover, get an injury, recover. But this one seems to be a lingering thing that has forced me to take a lot of time off and be patient. The funny thing, though, is that through this whole knee problem, even though I'm climbing less, I'm getting stronger. I think it's taught me that, "OK, there are a few things going on here."

On *The End of the Affair,* did you headpoint that?

Yeah. It's not had an onsight. It's almost a joke to place gear. You climb onto a boulder at the base, lean down, around the

Gritstone climbing really requires me to control my own mind when I'm climbing, to teach myself to relax if I'm scared.

corner place your gear, and then start climbing. It's basically a free solo up an arête. I know three people who have fallen off it. One time I went and looked at it, and there was blood on a rock at the bottom.

The headpointing style came about because bolting isn't allowed, and there are not that many natural features in the rock. At the same time, though, there are these beautiful lines that people wanted to climb. And quite often the moves are hard to read, so it's just not obvious climbing. It's powerful, yet delicate. For example, if your hips are 2 inches too far left, you'll fall. *The End of the Affair* is definitely like that—it's precarious the whole way up.

Since you're a boulderer, and since the gear was almost a joke, why even use a rope?

The gear does protect the bottom moves, and even though you shouldn't fall off there, you never know. If you go rigid, you're probably going to fall on it, so that did give me a sense of security. That route was actually a unique experience for me, because I do usually feel better when I take the rope off.

I just did another E7 last month, and it's basically a tall boulder problem. Unfortunately, however, the start is already high off the ground, so you definitely don't want to fall on the top. And it's been done different ways. Sometimes it's done by practicing on a rope and then soloing it, or some people lead it. So I kept debating whether or not I should lead it, and when I was working it, the rope was in my way, I was climbing really rigid, and I wasn't

enjoying it. When I took the toprope down, I just decided to solo it, and suddenly I climbed much more fluidly and freely. I guess, basically, every route is different.

Can you describe how you feel when you get to the top of a climb like that?

There is a certain adrenaline release. You're suppressing your adrenaline the whole time you're climbing, and then when you finish it's a huge relief. There's almost a sense of, "Oh good. I pulled it off." And of course there's that great feeling that you've accomplished something as well.

Have you gone through any times of no motivation?

I have. Right after I hurt my knee I had to pull out of World Cups, and I just felt that I couldn't climb how I wanted to. I wasn't using my legs properly because they hurt, and I felt like I was being pressured to do competitions in general. I just felt that if I couldn't do what I want to do, then why was I even climbing? I felt like I might as well get a job and go climbing on the weekends. And I seriously considered just quitting, getting a job, and climbing for myself. But even if I did that, everybody would still be watching me when I'd go to my local climbing area. I wouldn't stop being me. You can never just disappear again, so I thought, "OK, I love to climb. I love having the freedom, and I'm not going to complain about being in the public eye. Because that's what is allowing me to pursue what I want to do." So instead I just changed my focus and decided I wasn't

More Climbers to Watch

Angie Payne

Date of Birth: 11/6/84

Years Climbing: 10

Hometown: Cincinnati, Ohio

Known For: Bouldering

going to do all the competitions. And either people were going to be supportive or not. And I think that's made me feel more relaxed about my climbing.

Do you think that climbing as an occupation has changed your view of the sport or your desire for the sport?

With any job, it's a job. Fortunately mine is a fun job, but it's still a job. It changes your experience from "Let's just go on a climbing trip, party down, and hang out" to "OK, I actually need to be a bit careful with my diet, and I need to try to stretch and keep from getting injured." For example, I like mountain biking, but if I fall off and get hurt then I can't climb. I'm always thinking about that stuff. I have to be able to climb, that's part of being a professional climber, so I can't do something stupid that's going to keep me from being able to do that.

What are your goals or dreams?

Right now I feel like anything's possible. I feel like I have all these options but no focus, so I'm not actually making any plans. But I'd really like to have a climbing wall at home. We live in Bishop, and there's just nowhere to train in the winter. So I think we're going to go home and build a wall. I also want to start trying to get better at traditional climbing, so I'd like to start going to Tuolumne and the Sierras and just get some practice, so I relax more.

Why do you think traditional climbing interests you but sport doesn't?

Sport climbing is starting to interest me, but I've always liked multipitch climbing, and I like granite climbing. I guess I just like the lines that you see in traditional climbing. I probably need to go somewhere like Ceuse and get inspired. But when I was young, I'd go occasionally to Owens River Gorge, and there was nothing calling my

143

LISA RANDS

name. I've just not been interested in working a sport climb and seeing how hard I can redpoint. But that's kinda changing—I'm getting a bit curious to see if I can take my bouldering power, train some endurance, and then see what I can do.

Or just do really short sport climbs.

Yeah, but then you have to clip a bolt, and then if you miss it, you might hit the ground. There's this whole clipping problem, unfortunately.

Do you feel like having a rope is an obstruction to the purity of climbing then?

I'm not really looking at it from a viewpoint of what is pure and what is not. I'm not like that. It's more just that if I fall bouldering, my body orients in the air and I land on my feet on the ground. When I fall on a route, there's this rope, and I just swing.

How has pouring yourself into climbing affected your relationships?

I'm fortunate that Wills is very patient. I've become very controlling about where we go, and he just puts up with it. I think maybe it wouldn't work in a lot of relationships, so I'm fortunate. A lot of my friendships outside of climbing have totally suffered, though. I live this crazy lifestyle that's so different from what's considered normal in society. I sit down with old friends to have a conversation and they'll

say, "Oh, we just went to the river," and I'll say, "Oh, I just went to Russia." It's just difficult. With my family it's totally like that. I mean my great-uncle still asks me when I'm going to be ready for Everest.

Did you do a lot of sports or athletics before you got into climbing?

When I was real young I did gymnastics. Then I did track and field and cross-country, and then climbing. But I've always been a tomboy, just out there, being a tomboy, doing whatever we do, jumping out of trees and stuff.

Do you see yourself as a role model for younger climbers?

I hope so. I've always had a role model, so it's nice when people come up and tell me that I've inspired them. I see a lot more women out climbing now, and I hope that all of us women have helped influence them. I want women to go away from watching me climb realizing that we can be powerful and aggressive. We don't have to feel limited because we're women and we're not supposed to be that way.

Was there anyone in particular that was your role model?

Yeah. Lynn Hill. I started climbing right around the time she did *The Nose,* and it was such a huge thing. I thought it was amazing. I've pretty much always followed her climbing, and I just think she's had an amazing progression. She did the competition thing, then the sport climbing thing, then traditional climbing. And she's excelled at them all.

A while back I watched her onsight a 12c, and she was so relaxed. I thought, "Wow. That's what I need to learn to do." She'd go up and down trying to figure things out, then finally figure it out, and the rest of us would be too tired at that point to do the move. But she does it and looks totally solid and then keeps going.

Do you think that sort of inspiration has affected the path you've taken as a climber?

I think she's helped me realize that women can do things men can't do. I really do think that was a barrier with my climbing, and she's helped me realize it's not true. And also she's so positive. I remember a boulder problem in Moab that I didn't think I could do, and Lynn said, "Why not? Of course you can. You've done all the moves. Just rest and do it." And then I did it, but I had talked myself out of it at that point. It's just obvious that she loves climbing, and I think that's a great attitude to have, considering that she's so in the pub-

lic eye. You know because sometimes it can be hard when everyone's watching you, but it's as if she doesn't feel the pressure to perform. She's just out there to climb, and that's been really motivating.

How would you hope to be perceived by others?

I would hope that people would understand that I'm out there climbing because I love to climb. It's not because I'm a sponsored climber. That has come as a result of loving to climb. You know occasionally you have one of those days when you're grumpy and whining and you look around and realize that everybody's watching. Those are days when I hope people understand that I'm not really moody and weird. I'm just having a bad day. But that's something to remember. Somebody's always watching.

Do you think that you will always climb?

Oh yeah. I might not always be able to boulder, but I think I'll always be climbing.

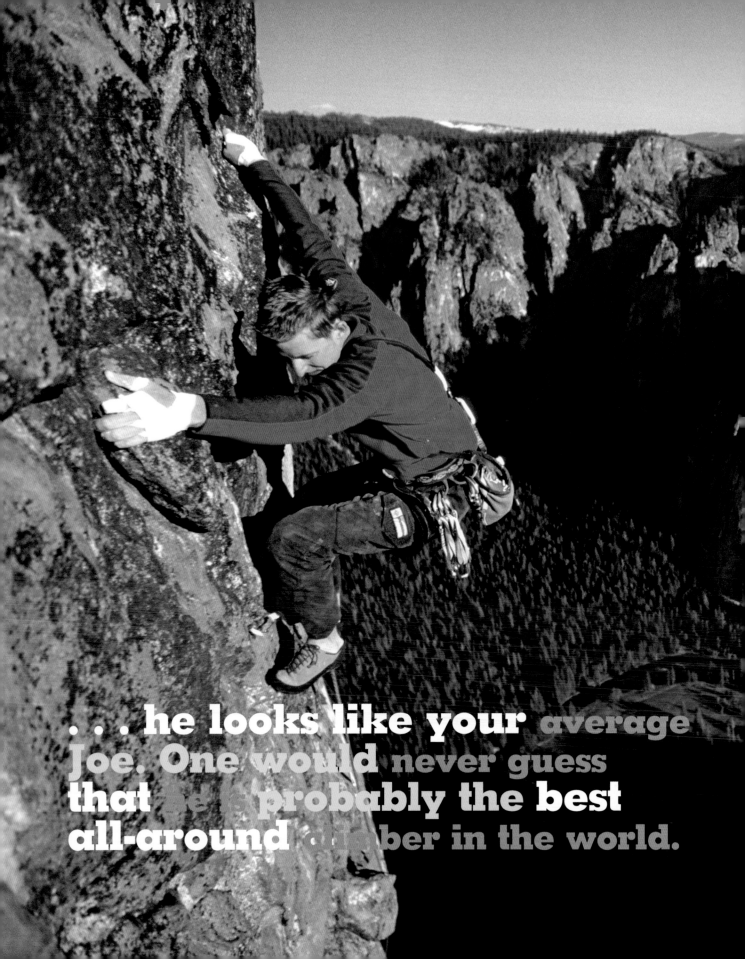

. . . he looks like your average Joe. One would never guess that he's probably the best all-around climber in the world.

Writes Tommy Caldwell for an *Alpinist* magazine article, "Growing up in Estes Park as the son of Mike Caldwell meant t-ball was for pansies, swimming was handy if you were caught in a flood, and an adventure wasn't an adventure without an unplanned bivy."

When asked how he started rock climbing, Tommy will tell you that he "climbed out of the womb." Unable to pinpoint when he was first introduced to climbing, his first memory of climbing, however, does involve flying a Superman kite. Today Tommy is of average height, with a slight build. He has a friendly face, complete with freckles and strawberry blonde hair. Aside from quite possibly being the only human to have 0 percent body fat, he looks like your average Joe. One would never guess that he is probably the best all-around climber in the world.

Tommy Caldwell is originally from Loveland, Colorado, but moved to Estes Park when he was young. Rock climbing had long been a passion of his dad's, and he passed that love for the sport down to his son. Growing up, Tommy spent nearly every weekend climbing in the summer, and skiing or camping in the winter. Rock climbing, however, was always top on the list of adventures, and Tommy had no reason to think that it was different for any other family.

By the time he was eleven, Tommy was the youngest person to climb the Diamond on Longs Peak, and by fourteen, he had been to Bolivia to climb two 20,000-foot peaks. It was in the early 1990s, however, when sport climbing really began taking off, that Tommy truly found his own identity in climbing. After helping to develop a new sport climbing area, called The Monastery, Tommy discovered that he had a passion for finding and establishing new lines. That quest led through his teens and early twenties, as he and his father found and established numerous classic, difficult lines, including Estes's first 5.14, *Sarchasm*.

By 2000 Tommy longed to take his skills to new testing ground and decided that Yosemite Valley and El Cap would be the perfect place. El Cap would prove to be just that, as well as the place where we would meet his future wife, Beth Rodden. Since that first trip to Yosemite, Tommy has free-climbed numerous routes on El Cap, including the world's most difficult big wall free climb, the *Dihedral Wall,* and the most famous route on El Cap, *The Nose*.

Tommy Caldwell

Height: **5 feet, 10 inches**

Weight: **150 pounds**

Date of Birth: **8/11/78**

Current Hometown: **Estes Park, Colorado**

Age of First Climb: **3**

Approximate Number of Days Per Year Spent Climbing: **200**

Hardest Climb: **Number-wise—*Flex Luther* (15a); Effort-wise—*Dihedral Wall* (14a); Commitment-wise: *Linea de Eleganza*, Patagonia (12d)**

Favorite Climbing Area: **Yosemite**

The Interview . . .

How did you start climbing?

The first time that I can actually remember was on Twin Owls, here in Estes. On the backside there's a fourth class, pitch and a half route. I didn't want to go because of the climbing, I wanted to go because my dad had bribed me by saying that I could fly a Superman kite off the top, so that's all I was excited about. I just liked getting up high and throwing things off the top.

How old were you?

Three. The first time I climbed *Half Dome*—and the only reason I climbed it, I swear—was because I wanted to throw this little paper airplane that we had bought at the valley store off the top.

You were raised to do a lot of different athletic things. Why'd you choose climbing above the others?

I wasn't really raised to do anything but climb.

But you went skiing and running and biking, and backpacking . . .

Yeah. We were active, but the focus was always climbing, which is probably why I picked it above the others. And plus I just sucked at anything else. I was really bad at team sports. I was OK at stuff where you could just suffer it out, but any sports that involved teamwork or coordination . . .

Did you go climbing mostly with your dad?

Yeah. It was good. He was always super-excited about climbing, so that's probably where I got a lot of it. He probably has more energy and excitement than pretty much anybody when it comes to climbing.

What was it about climbing that you liked?

I like a lot of things about it. I like being out in the mountains and getting to go to amazing places. It gives you a good excuse to travel and see the world—and in a way that only climbers get to do. It brings you to places that not all tourists would go. And the challenge of it—I thrive on things that really push me. I'm somebody who finds something to focus on—some goal—and then I work toward that. And climbing is perfect for that.

When did you start moving away from climbing with your dad?

Probably when I met Beth. My dad was my main climbing partner until then. I mean I climbed with other people, but he was still my main partner.

Did you ever think about going to college?

Yeah, I thought about it. I graduated from high school thinking I would go to college in a year. But that summer I spent two months in Europe, and I just couldn't imagine sitting in a classroom after getting back from having the time of my life. I just didn't think I could deal with it. So at first I said that I was just going to postpone it a year, but the years kept passing and the climbing just started working out better and better.

What kind of climbing did you mainly do when you were younger?

I started out mainly climbing in Vedauwoo and on Lumpy Ridge, crack climbing and slabs mostly, which is rare for a little kid. But then once I started climbing for me, instead of just with the family, it was mostly sport climbing for a long time.

Is there a genre of climbing that you like over all the others?

I think it changes all the time, but right now it's more adventure climbing and big wall free climbing—specifically, on El Cap. Gotta find your niche (laughs). It's the only

Tommy at his home crag,
The Monastery, Colorado

Tommy running it out, sideways, on *The West Buttress*, El Capitan, Yosemite National Park, California

way to make it as a professional climber. It's not about climbing hard, it's just about finding your niche.

So how did you end up doing the competition circuit?

Well when I was in middle school, my dad had a climbing program, and that's probably what got me into indoor climbing. Since I had been climbing since I was little, I was pretty good at it, so we started going to climbing gyms as well. And from there, what's the next step? You go to comps. The national circuit was pretty big back then, so I decided to do those. I had been working as a busboy in the summer ever since I was eleven, and I started to realize that I could go to comps and make enough money that I didn't have to bus tables as much.

And how did you like the comps?

I put tons of pressure on myself. I was miserable, actually. I never had fun at the comps. It was a way to push myself, and I liked training for the comps and feeling stronger, but I almost liked the training part and the psyche that comps gave me more than the comps themselves. I mean I don't know if I put as much pressure on myself as you guys did, but I never climbed as good in the comps as I did out cragging, because I was too nervous. And I wasn't good with nervousness I guess—although now in big wall climbing I can do thirty pitches and think, "OK, I gotta do this pitch now or the whole day, the whole month, is wasted." And I can climb better then. But it's different for some reason.

Why do you think it's different?

Maybe it's more of an internal, personal pressure rather than trying to please everyone around me and trying to put on a show.

How has your relationship with Beth affected your goals?

It's been really good. I don't know if she was as goal oriented as me before we met, but she seems to have taken that attitude a little bit, which helps push me further. Also I've got an incredibly reliable partner, which is really hard to find. And I'm not just doing it for me. Climbing is very selfish, but being able to do it for Beth and with Beth helps a lot.

What accomplishment are you the most proud of?

Scoring Beth.

You do realize this is going in a book?

Yes.

So how do you think Kyrgyzstan has changed you as a person or as a climber?

For a while I felt that since we had lived through it, we needed to make every day count—and maybe that still applies. After Kyrgyzstan, and after cutting off my finger, I was always supermotivated, pushing really hard because I felt like I needed to live life to its fullest. Life just seemed a little more tangible and not as permanent after Kyrgyzstan.

Do you think an experience like that has actually helped your climbing?

Yeah. Absolutely. It's made me tougher. I mean it was hard obviously, but going through hard things can make you tougher. And especially the kind of climbing we do now, being tough is important.

What was it like coming back from cutting your finger off? Did you have any doubts that you'd be able to climb like you did before?

At first, for sure. I was really worried about it in the hospital. I just thought, "My life has been climbing. Everything I've done, everything I've worked toward. And I don't know if I'm going to be able to do it at anywhere near the level that I did before." But I guess I just wasn't willing to accept that, so even before I got out of the hospital, I was really determined to come back. For six months or so after the injury, I trained harder than ever—I just wasn't going to let it slow me down, and I think now I climb stronger and better because of it.

Why did you choose the *Dihedral Wall*? Was it the only thing left on El Cap that you hadn't already freed?

It was the next most obvious option. It seems like we spend a good portion of our

life sitting in the meadow looking up at El Cap, and from there it's a really obvious line. Todd Skinner and Paul Piana had tried it, so I knew that there was maybe a chance that it would go. At first I just took the approach that I take with all the routes on El Cap, I just went up to do reconnaissance. I actually soloed it as an aid route to see if I really thought it would go and it looked amazing, so . . .

What do you think makes it so much harder than other routes on El Cap?

It's much more sustained, and there are no ledges. All the pitches are hard, from beginning to the end. Some of the other routes might have moves that are as hard or almost as hard, but the *Dihedral Wall* is just amazingly sustained.

In your article you were talking about feeling for the first time in your life like you couldn't go on. How did you cope with that feeling or level of exhaustion?

I got to a point where I was almost numb to it. Usually when you're training, you climb, get tired, and start to feel a drop in strength. On the *Dihedral Wall* I went through that process several times. I'd drop off, then get a second wind that I'd never really pushed through before, then get through that, and on and on. I got to a point where I was just quivering and in so much pain. And I guess it's just the same thing—you get another wind, but at that point your body's numb.

Holding onto noth-
ing on the *Dihedral
Wall*, El Capitan,
Yosemite National
Park, California

What do you think drives you to push yourself that hard?

I don't know. I'm probably too obsessive. A flaw in the gene pool. I don't know.

Do you enjoy the process of it, or do you enjoy the feeling that you get afterward?

Probably more the process. I just like seeing how far I can take it, I think. And climbing on big walls puts you in an environment that enables you to push through things that would be too painful otherwise.

Why?

Because there's more distraction. For example, if you're sitting in your house and you take a razor blade and start scraping away the skin on your fingers, it would hurt like crazy. But that's basically what you do when you're climbing, and it's no problem. You can climb until your fingertips bleed, and it doesn't hurt that bad.

How did you feel after finishing the *Dihedral Wall*?

At first I was ecstatic. I mean I had worked really hard at that climb. But I would say if that was the only reason that I did it, then I probably wouldn't be able to do it. It wouldn't be worth it. It's about the process and seeing how far you can push yourself. It's not really about the accomplishment or the feeling you get right afterward.

Have you thought of doing the *Dihedral Wall* in a day?

Well it's always something that could potentially be in the back of my mind.

You guys recently did a second free ascent of *The Nose*. Why do you think *The Nose* hasn't been repeated before now? What sets it apart?

Historically, routes that are hard for the grade do not get repeated. Other routes on El Cap have the same or even a harder number grade but are much easier. Also, the climbing on the Changing Corners pitch is bizarre and unlike anything else I have climbed. It took a lot of dedication to figure out how to climb it.

The crowds are also a big concern. We were careful not to get in the way of aid climbers, because we want everyone to have a pure experience on El Cap without having to deal with our fixed ropes, etcetera. That was not easy and caused a lot more work for us. It would have been easy to get frustrated and give up on it altogether, but we realized that it wasn't going to get any less crowded.

What was the most challenging part for you?

In terms of the climbing, the Changing Corners pitch was far harder than anything else on the route. Freeing that many pitches in a push is also always a big challenge, no matter what. For me, the key to freeing something on El Cap is efficiency and an ability to be ultraproductive. This means you have to climb all day many days in a row. It puts you through a lot of pain,

It's about
the process
and seeing
how **far you**
can push
yourself.

and you have to push through your comfort zone all the time.

What was the most challenging part for you as a team?

Having Beth as the other part of the team is the only reason I could free *The Nose* in the first place. Team free ascents, where both free every pitch, is a very demanding way to climb. It's much harder than leading every pitch with a partner who jugs behind you and does all the manual labor. It compounds the logistics and adds a lot of extra work.

How did it feel to repeat such a historical route?

It was a superlofty goal for us. We were never confident that we would be able to pull it off, so when we topped out it was surreal. We couldn't believe that we actually had been able to do it.

How do you mentally approach a task as big as freeing a route on El Cap?

I don't think of it like that. I don't think of it as, "I'm going to go free climb this route." I think of it as, "I'm going to go try and see what happens." I mean at some point during the process I realize that maybe I'll be able to do it, and then it becomes a real goal. But I'm never thinking that at first. Then it would probably be a little overwhelming. On the *Dihedral Wall* I decided first to solo it, because I had never soloed a wall before. That was the first step. And then I figured I'd go try the first five pitches, and that was the next step. I break it down that way.

You've been climbing for your whole life. Have you ever not been motivated or felt burned out?

No, not really. I mean there are times when

More Climbers to Watch

Matt Segal

Date of Birth: 5/8/84

Years Climbing: 7

Hometown: Miami, Florida

Known For: Up and coming all-around climber; first ascent of *Iron Monkey* (5.14a), Eldorado Canyon, Colorado

I feel a little burned out, but I think it helps that I really like all the different kinds of climbing. If I only bouldered, I'd definitely burn out. But if I get tired of bouldering, I can go sport climbing or big wall climbing. It always keeps it fresh. In fact I almost feel like the seasons make me alternate more quickly than I want to, so I'm always psyched about what I'm doing. Especially with all the other stuff that we do now, as far as being a professional climber, there's probably less time to climb, so I'm even more excited to do it.

What do you see next for yourself?

I still have different ideas about routes on El Cap. I'm not tired of that yet. I'm excited to go to Patagonia and Baffin. I'd like to do a little bit of alpine climbing, but probably not tons. I don't think I'm going to become a full-on expedition climber who just leaves his wife at home for months on end, because that always ends in divorce.

Is there anyone that you look up to?

My dad, for a long time. He was probably the main one.

What would you hope to pass on to younger climbers who will be reading this book?

Younger climbers need to make sure they're climbing for the right reasons. I mean maybe I'm just getting old and bitter, but it seems like for a lot of younger climbers their big goal is to get sponsored or to

shock their friends. But climbing is so much more than that—it can be a way to do all kinds of amazing things, like I said before when you asked me why I liked climbing.

I mean my whole life is about climbing, but I don't think that's necessarily the best way to be. You know, people shouldn't focus too much on it because . . . I mean it works for me, but it might not for other people.

How would you like to be viewed by other people?

I'd like people to know that I'm genuine and real.

159

TOMMY CALDWELL

Photographers

Jimmy Chin

Jimmy lives in Jackson, Wyoming. He has worked all over the world for publications such as *Outside, National Geographic,* and *Men's Journal.* Not only a photographer, however, Jimmy is also an accomplished climber himself. Some of his accomplishments include summiting Mount Everest and climbing the world's tallest freestanding sandstone towers in Mali, Africa. www.jimmychinphotography.com

Jonathan Copp

Jonathan has had his passport stolen by a monkey in India, been given a test run with a machine gun in Pakistan, been robbed in Reno, and has starved in Patagonia. He is known for high-level alpinism and has made impressive first ascents worldwide, including the first-ever alpine style ascent of a Grade VII. He's been the recipient of a number of grants to fund explorations. Jonathan's photography and writing have been published in magazines, journals, books, and film. www.coppworks.com.

Kelly Cordes

Kelly didn't start climbing until the age of twenty-five, while in graduate school in Montana. Today he enjoys and excels at lightweight alpinism, including being Josh Wharton's partner in crime on the *Azeem Ridge* of the Great Trango Tower. He currently lives in Estes Park, Colorado, and works part-time as the assistant editor of the *American Alpine Journal.*

Topher Donahue

Topher lives in Nederland, Colorado, with girlfriend and fellow climber Vera Schultze-Pelkum. He has been taking photographs for many years but has also been featured as a climber in films such as *Front Range Freaks* and *Parallelojams.* Look for Topher's first ascents in places like the Bugaboos, the Diamond on Longs Peak, the Black Canyon of the Gunnison, and elsewhere. You can also find his photography in the likes of *Sports Illustrated, Outside,* and *Ski* magazine.
www.alpinecreative.com

Dean Fidelman

Dean has been taking photos for more than thirty years. He was perhaps one of the original Yosemite "monkeys" and still spends as much time as possible bumming around the valley, soaking up sun and granite. Dean works solely in black-and-white and is best known for his series of calendars entitled "Stone Nudes."

PatitucciPhoto

PatitucciPhoto is the unique combination of the husband and wife team of Dan and Janine Patitucci. Splitting their time between homes in Bishop, California and Luzern, Switzerland allows them to photograph in many different mountain environments. The images they produce are a result of their energetic and creative passion for the sports themselves.
www.patitucciphoto.com

Eric Perlman

Eric has been a climber, writer, photographer and filmmaker for more than 30 years and is known for the *Masters of Stone* videos.

Corey Rich

At only twenty-nine, Corey is one of the most widely recognized adventure photographers in the industry. He currently calls Lake Tahoe, California, home and works maniacally for clients such as Anheuser-Busch, Nike, Advil, and TNF in between sessions of climbing, snowboarding, or surfing.
www.coreyrich.com

Whit Richardson

Whit, originally from Boulder, Colorado, currently lives in Moab, Utah, where he is able to pursue both his passion for photography and his passion for the outdoors. If not in his office, he can be found out backcountry skiing or climbing desert cracks. Look for Whit's work not only in many popular publications, but also framed and available for purchase as fine art landscape prints.
www.whitrichardson.com

Boone Speed

Boone is originally from the mountains of Utah. He discovered climbing in 1985 and before long had established several sport routes that were, at the time, the hardest in America. Boone has been a driving force within the climbing community for many years, and his influence includes designs for shoes, gear, and climbing holds. His photography has also been published in climbing magazines worldwide.

Other Contributors

Ally Dorey, Chris Goplerud, Tim Kemple and Sonnie Trotter

Thanks to all our photographers for providing such excellent work!

PHOTOGRAPHERS

About the Author

As the first woman to onsight 5.13d (*Omaha Beach*, Red River Gorge, Kentucky) and flash 5.14a (*Hydrophobia*, Mont Sant, Spain), **Katie Brown** has been an influential and groundbreaking climber. She began climbing at age thirteen and quickly dominated competition at the national and international level. Now in her early twenties, she is a freelance writer and continues to travel the world as a professional climber.